Keys to Effective Motivation

Keys to Effective Motivation

Reginald M. McDonough

BROADMAN PRESS
Nashville, Tennessee

4232-26

ISBN: 0-8054-3226-4

Dewey Decimal Classification: 254

Subject headings: CHURCH WORK//MOTIVATION (PSYCHOLOGY)

Library of Congress Catalog Card Number: 77-26532

Printed in the United States of America

Preface

Ask a church leader what his most perplexing challenge is and he will likely say, "How can I motivate the folks I work with?" Apathy and nonparticipation by Christians is the curse of the church today, just as it was when the apostle John penned the Revelation. When a church catches on fire spiritually, no goal is too large, no challenge too great. But too often the fire is not present and victory is lost. Jesus said, "O Jerusalem, Jerusalem, who kills the prophets and stones those who are sent to her! How often I wanted to gather your children together, the way a hen gathers her chicks under her wings, and you were unwilling" (Matt. 23:37, *New American Standard Bible*).[1]

Every minister has felt this despair in his heart because many of those he leads are not involved in the mission. This book is about the dilemma of non-involvement.

No easy answers will be offered. In fact, as will be explained more fully in chapter 5, I do not believe a leader can control the motivation of those he leads. He seeks to provide a climate in which persons can motivate themselves, and he supports them in prayer.

Let's also shoot straight about what the book is not. It is not a catalog of sure-fire gimmicks for manipulating people. Unfortunately, too many church leaders think manipulative gimmickery is synonymous with building a climate for healthy motivation.

The purpose of this volume is threefold: (1) to help church leaders understand the dynamics of motivation, (2) to expose the shortcomings of manipulation, and (3) to share some of the key ingredients for building a climate in which persons will be motivated.

The essence of leadership is helping persons become motivated. This is the great desire of every church leader. It is my belief that every leader can be effective in helping persons become motivated. It is a myth to believe that only an outgoing, smooth-talking person with good platform skills can help persons be highly motivated. In fact, the keys to effective motivation relate more to attitudes and positive actions than to personality traits. In this arena of leadership, as in any other, a leader should seek to extend his strengths, not copy another person's style.

The nature of Christian motivation is another subject that needs early clarification. Some persons try to divide a person's motivation into three parts: physical, psychological, and spiritual. I must admit that I tried to do this at one time. But to do this implies that physical and psychological needs of persons are not spiritual.

It was a great day when I admitted that God made all of me. While it is true that a part of me is mystical, all of my needs are available to the Holy Spirit. God can and does work through all my needs. The distinctive of Christian motivation is a Christian's relationship to God through the Holy Spirit, not some special compartment in his life that is reserved for spiritual motives.

I actually wrote the first chapter last. My original intention was to deal only with manipulation and motivation. But I continually bumped into the Christian doctrine of man. It became apparent to me that a leader's theology of man is foundational to how he relates to people. It is the belief that man is God's marvelous creation that makes manipulation off limits. The doctrine of man is the beginning point for studying manipulation and motivation. This study was a rich experience for me. Like Moses, I felt I was on holy ground. I would encourage you to do a more extensive study than I have presented.

I have leaned heavily on the work of Abraham Maslow. Very little of Maslow's work was original. He borrowed heavily from many psychological schools of thought. This is the genius of his work. He pulled the work of many into a package that makes sense to me. I am indebted to two of his colleagues, Frank Goble and Colin Wilson, for their commentaries on Maslow's work that made it even more understandable and applicable.

The work of Everett Shostrom was significantly helpful in the study of manipulation. His book *Man, the Manipulator* is a classic and the source of many of the ideas I have presented.

I would also like to pay tribute to my colleagues in the Church Administration Department of the Sunday School Board. They are a constant source of inspiration and challenge to me. I would especially like to thank Wanda Harris and Jean Merritt, who helped me greatly in the preparation of the manuscript.

My family—Joan, Mike, and Teri—have also contributed greatly to this volume. Not only have they allowed me to isolate myself for many hours to do this writing; they constantly demonstrate that persons are God's marvelous creations.

To me, faith in God, faith in oneself, faith in others, and prayer are the mystical ingredients in Christian motivation. These do not negate the scientific data we have collected about the nature of man. These Christian dimensions of leadership simply put all that we do or try to do in proper perspective. This book is dedicated to all those fellow pilgrims who are seeking to lead God's children to the promised lands of joy and effective Christian discipleship.

Contents

Part I
Man, God's Marvelous Creation

Man is God's marvelous creation, crowned with glory and honor, and because of this you can't quite hem him in. You can put him in Bedford's prison, but somehow his mind will break out through the bars to scratch across the pages of history a *Pilgrim's Progress.* You can bring him down in his wretched old age, with his body broken down and his vision all but gone, and yet in the form of a Handel, he will look up and imagine that he hears the very angels singing, and he will come back and scratch across the pages of history a "Hallelujah Chorus."

This is man. He is God's marvelous creation.[2]

—*Martin Luther King, Jr.*

1
A Biblical
View of Man

"When I look at the sky, which you have made, at the moon and the stars, which you set in their places— what is man, that you think of him; mere man, that you care for him: Yet you have made him inferior only to yourself; you crowned him with glory and honor. You appointed him ruler over everything you made; you placed him over all creation: sheep and cattle; and the wild animals too; the birds and the fish and the creatures in the seas" (Ps. 8:3-8, TEV).[3]

What tremendous worth! Although man's worth in terms of the minerals in his body is only a few dollars, his value is priceless in God's economy. If God holds persons in such high esteem, certainly Christian leaders should seek the same attitude. Persons should value themselves highly and resist the temptation to treat other persons as things to be used. In terms of motivation and manipulation the supreme value of persons is a vital basic concept.

The scientists have provided invaluable data in understanding God's creation—the human personality. These insights will be used extensively in this book. But it would be foolish to attempt to formulate a Christian philosophy of motivation without dealing with the biblical view of man. All we do as Christian leaders should be consistent with a sound theology of man. Man is God's marvelous creation.

Made the Crown of Creation

God's creative process reaches its zenith in the creation of man. The earlier verses of Genesis 1 tell of God's creation of the heavenly bodies, the earth, the plants, the animals, the birds, and the fish. Each time God said that it was good. But when God created man, he gave him dominion over all the earth and everything on it. E. Y. Mullins states that "we cannot understand the creation except by viewing it as a whole. Man is its crown and good. Looking forward from the last state prior to man we should expect man to appear." [4]

Created in the Image of God

As if it weren't enough to give man a place at the apex of creation, God created man in his own image. Genesis 1:27 records that "God created man in His image, in the image of God he created him: male and female He created them" (NASB).

What does it mean to be created in the image of God? Are we physically like God? William Hendrix explains the view held by many scholars:

"If God were physical [as we are], how could he be present in all times and places (Ps. 139)? Christian theology must not picture people as puppets cut from a master pattern of a physical God. Nor can we imagine God as a vision of a human merely drawn to a larger scale. A more acceptable view of the image of God in man is that the image is a person's reasoning ability." [5]

It is man's ability to reason that sets him apart from God's other creations. The Scriptures say, "Come now, and let us reason together" (Isa. 1:18).

Man's relationship to God's image is also seen in his emotional, volitional, and social characteristics.

As an emotional being, man is capable of feeling. The ability to feel gives a person the capacity to love. Without this capacity man could not relate meaningfully to himself, others, and God.

The volitional capacity of man gives him the ability to will. This capacity transcends the physical. It gives persons the ability to project meaning.

The social nature of persons gives the ability to relate meaningfully to other God-created persons as social beings and to have fellowship with one another.

Being created in the image of God means that persons can be proud of who they are. As someone has said, "God didn't make no junk." Not all of a person's deeds are good, but being created in the image of God gives the "potentiality, ability, and responsibility to respond to God, the self, and others." [6]

In terms of Christian motivation, the capacity that results from a person's likeness to God is the heart of the self-determination theory of motivation. Within each person is the capacity to think, feel, and become.

Given the Freedom of Choice

Freedom means that God did not make man a puppet on a string. He has the freedom of self-determination. His actions are not predetermined by external forces.

But with his freedom comes responsibility.

Mullins expresses this idea forcefully: "Freedom does not imply exemption from the operation of influences, motives, heredity, environment. It means rather that man is not under compulsion. His actions are in the last resort determined from within." [7]

Persons have the freedom to choose good or evil. Otherwise, a person's worship of God would be worthless. Love and adoration are meaningless if they are not given of a person's own free will. Although this God-given privilege gives persons a tremendous opportunity, it carries with it a tremendous risk and responsibility. It means that man must be responsible for his acts.

The act of marriage illustrates the concept of freedom and responsibility. In the United States, two adult persons are free to get married. They exercise their freedom to do so. But when they enter the marriage relationship, a responsibility to the other partner must be assumed. If no commitment and no mutual responsibility exist, the relationship has no meaning and will fall apart. All meaningful relationships are built on the premise of mutual freedom and responsibility. This attribute of man is further evidence of man's place at the zenith of God's creation.

In the Garden of Eden, Adam and Eve were given the freedom of choice; but they had a responsibility to obey God. Because they were responsible for their actions, they had to bear the consequences of their actions when they disobeyed God.

The biblical concept of freedom has a two-sided implication for Christian leaders. First, the concept of individual freedom to act means that a church leader does not, in fact cannot, accept responsibility for the behavior of those he seeks to lead. He can aid and encourage them, but he cannot become responsible for them. Jesus grieved over the city of Jerusalem, but he did not take responsibility for the people's behavior. That responsibility belonged to the people of Jerusalem, just as persons today are responsible to God for their behavior.

The other implication of the biblical concept of freedom relates to the source of motivation. Because God made man free to choose, the ultimate source of motivation springs from within each person. To be motivated toward a particular cause is a decision that each person can make, indeed must make, for himself.

Relationships Broken and Restored

Man is created in the image of God, the crown of his creation with dominion over the earth, and is given the freedom to choose; but this is just part of the picture.

The biblical picture of man is not complete without exploring man's response to his freedom and God's promises for restoring the broken relationship.

Marred by Sin

Man had been created to have close fellowship with God. Genesis 3:8 implies that God had direct fellowship with man before he disobeyed Him. But in God's wisdom he had given man the freedom of choice. Man chose to disobey God—sin. Thus, by his own choice man cast aside his special relationship to God. He failed to live up to the full potential that God had placed in him.

Not only did Adam, the first man, choose to cast aside his special relationship to God; but also all men since Adam, as a result of a sinful disposition, have followed his pattern. In Romans 3:23 Paul wrote, "All have sinned." Several theories are generally held about the origin of sin, but that is not important here. The fact is that all persons are sinners. They have chosen to compete with God. Man's own egocentricity continues to be his undoing.

The experience of Adam helps us understand man's behavior today.

The temptation and the fall are repeated in the lives of persons many times each day. Persons rebel against God and fall short of the wholeness that was created in them. Fallen man hides from God and seeks to blame other persons for his plight.

"Our freedom," says William Hendrix, "has produced evil which causes both us and God to suffer . . . . The step from innocence to responsibility involves both man and God. We have not carried the weight of our responsibility well. But God has remained true to his responsibility for creation." [8]

James Mallory tells the story of a preacher who announced he had completed an exhaustive study of sin and had catalogued every sin in existence. As he delivered his message, he waved the list of eighty-six commonly known and obscure sins before the congregation. After the service he was besieged by persons who wanted a copy of the list to see what they might have missed.

Man's rebellion and sin have several implications regarding Christian motivation. Man is not a predictable creature. He is influenced by both God and Satan. Paul said, "I am a mortal man, sold as a slave to sin. I do not understand what I do; for I don't do what I would like to do, but instead I do what I hate" (Rom. 7:14-15, TEV). It is a colossal mistake for a leader to believe he can "figure out" a person or group of persons. Helping others become motivated is an art, not a science.

Another very important motivational implication of man's fallen state is the effect of his self-worship on his behavior. Man is a self-centered creature. As a general rule, a person gives his needs first priority. Manipulation of self and others comes easy. Self-sacrifice is difficult.

But man's high esteem of himself is not altogether problematic. It is this sense of self-worth that enables a person to celebrate his gifts and relate meaningfully to others. The Scriptures say: "Love your neighbor as yourself." Self-love, then, is a model for loving others. Only when a person carries his sense of self-worth to excess does it become detrimental.

Man is certainly God's marvelous creation. From a potentially destructive tendency, he shapes a wonderful strength.

Redeemed by Love

"For sin pays its wages—death; but God's free gift is eternal life in union with Christ Jesus our Lord" (Rom. 6:23, TEV).

God's relationship to man is such a beautiful picture.

He exalted man by creating him in his own image and by giving him dominion over the earth. He honored man by giving him the freedom to choose good or evil. And, because in his omnipotent knowledge he knew man would cast aside his perfect relationship, he extended his great love toward him by making a way for fallen man to restore the relationship.

It is extremely significant to note that God took the initiative to search out Adam and Eve after they had sinned. God's first communication was, "Where are you?" (Gen. 1:9, TEV). This stance has continued to be God's attitude toward man. John 3:16 says, "For God loved the world so much that he gave his only Son, so that everyone who believes in him may not die but have eternal life" (TEV).

In the Old Testament God provided a sacrificial system to "make atonement" for sin and remove the barrier between God and man. But atonement in the Old Testament always looked forward to the perfect sacrifice in Jesus Christ. In Jesus Christ, God demonstrated a love that conquered sin and death. "God offered him, so that by his death he should become the means by which people's sins are forgiven through their faith in him" (Rom. 3:25, TEV).

Because of God's great love for man, he has made a way to forgive him and restore the fellowship that was marred by man's sin. But God does not force his gift on man. Man has the option to accept or reject his love.

This facet of the doctrine of man is also extremely significant regarding human motivation. God's provi sion for restoring fellowship with man has given man the capacity to transcend egocentricity and recapture in his personality the Godlike traits of love and forgiveness. It is the fact that sinful persons can and do respond to God's love that gives a Christian leader great hope and challenge.

Reaffirmed by Jesus

Jesus not only made possible man's salvation but also reaffirmed through his teachings the focus of God's love for man. Many of his parables and figures of speech illustrate God's love and care for man. Matthew quoted Jesus as saying, "Yet not one sparrow falls to the ground without your Father's consent. As for you, even the hairs of your head have all been counted. So do not be afraid; you are worth much more than many sparrows" (Matt. 10:29-31, TEV).

Jesus tells the parable of the prodigal son who rejects his father's love and squanders his inheritance but is welcomed back to the father's household and returned to fellowship in the family. God, he says, is like a shepherd who, when one sheep is lost, leaves the others to find the one that was lost. He gives the assurance that he and the Father are one and that no man can take away a person who is securely in his hand. Jesus leaves no doubt that man is the crown of God's creation—a marvelous creation.

2
Man's Many Needs

Marge Brown is a fifth-grade schoolteacher. She has received many awards for her teaching excellence. In fact, just about any pupil or parent related to the Stanford Elementary School would tell you that Mrs. Brown is the best teacher in the school. Marge is also an active member of the Brook Hollow Church. Ed Porter has recently come to the Brook Hollow Church as pastor and is facing his first year of working with the church's nominating committee. Already Marge's reputation as an expert teacher has reached Ed. He cannot believe his ears when the nominating committee tells him that Mrs. Brown will not take the position as fifth-grade department director. When he confronts her himself, her response is: "Brother Porter, thanks for asking me to serve. I love fifth graders, but Sunday morning I desperately need to be with my own age group. Can't you find me a place to serve in my adult department?"

Sound familiar? Why does Mrs. Brown not want to work with fifth graders when she is so skilled in teaching this age? Why is she willing to risk rejection by her new pastor by refusing to take the department? Does she really need to be with adults that much? What is causing her to behave this way?

The answer to all these questions can be summed up in one word—needs. Mrs. Brown has an unsatisfied need that she feels can only be met by being with adults on Sunday morning. Apparently her needs for achievement and affirmation are met by her schoolteaching, but the need to be accepted by adult friends is not. There are any number of other possibilities why she needs to be not with the fifth graders on Sunday but with adults. The reason is not important here. Nor is it necessary to judge the quality of her decision. What is important is to realize that Mrs. Brown is acting on the basis of her felt needs.

Needs are the mainsprings of behavior. Needs provide the pulls that cause a person to act as he does. They may not be observable or even consciously known to the individual, but they exist. The strength of needs varies greatly according to the environment, cultural conditions, and a person's ability to satisfy his needs. Although the complexity of a person's need structure makes it impossible to fully analyze why persons act as they do, an understanding of human needs is essential to effective leadership.

This chapter will seek to examine five categories of needs that are felt to some extent by all persons: physiological needs, safety needs, social needs, esteem needs, and growth needs.

Physiological Needs

Physiological needs are man's most basic needs. They are the innate, biogenic needs which stimulate

a person to preserve life and health. The existence of
these needs is well established and calls for only brief
treatment.

Hunger and Thirst.—Food and drink in sufficient
amounts are absolutely essential to sustain life.

Rest and Sleep.—A person cannot function efficiently
without sufficient rest and sleep.

Elimination.—The elimination of liquid and solid
wastes is essential to the health of a person.

Respiration.—The intake of oxygen through breath-
ing the air is clearly essential to sustain life.

Sexual Gratification.—This need exists in persons
from their early years, but becomes highly significant
from puberty onward.

Intermediate Temperature.—A person cannot live
long in an environment that does not allow his system
to function normally.

Pain Avoidance.—This need relates to a person's
need to have a sense of general well-being and to avoid
hurt.

Although each of these physiological needs exists
in each person, their relative significance may be condi-
tional by culture and individual values.

Physiological needs are generally satisfied outside
the church. However, such conveniences as meals, air
conditioning, rest rooms, and water fountains are some
of the ways that churches acknowledge the motivational strengths of these needs. Also, it should be noted
that the satisfaction of many of the physiological needs
is intricately linked with physio-social needs. It is very
difficult, for example, to say that a person is only satis-

fying his need for food at a church meal. The need for fellowship (belonging) may be equally strong.

Significantly, however, a person whose physiological needs are not being met to his satisfaction will not respond to incentives based on higher needs. A starving man has little or no concern for ego.

Safety Needs

Another category of needs that motivate persons relates to safety. These needs generally emerge if a person's physiological needs are relatively well met. Abraham Maslow describes the safety category as the need for security; stability; dependency; protection; freedom from fear, anxiety, and chaos; structure; order; law; limits; and strength in the protector.[9]

Saul W. Gellerman indicates that a person's conscious safety needs also play a background role, often inhibiting or restraining impulses rather than initiating outward behavior.[10]

Safety needs play a significant role in a person's decision to become a Christian. It is through a person's felt need for eternal security that the Holy Spirit often works to bring a person to repentance and faith.

A person's response to change and new information is another area where safety needs come into play. Persons generally prefer the familiar to the unfamiliar. For example, one reason why many adults do not want to change Bible study classes as they progress in age can be traced to their need for safety. The new environment is a threat to their needs for stability, structure, and order. A wise church leader will seek to reduce the threat of instability when suggesting changes. The positive side of this need will be treated fully in a later chapter.

Maslow summarizes this need succinctly: "The average adult in our society generally prefers a safe, orderly, predictable, lawful, organized world, which he can count on and in which unexpected, unmanageable, chaotic, or other dangerous things do not happen, and in which he, in any case, has powerful parents or protectors who shield him from harm." [11] This statement speaks volumes to the church leader who is seeking to build a climate in which persons can generate and sustain a high level of motivation.

Social Needs

Man is a social being. He needs to love and be loved. He needs to interact with other persons, to feel accepted, and to belong. Solitary confinement has long been regarded as the most severe punishment in the penal system short of death.

Maslow states that a person "will want to attain such a place [group or family] more than anything else in the world and may even forget that once, when he was hungry, he sneered at love as unreal or unnecessary or unimportant. Now he will feel sharply the pangs of loneliness, of ostracism, of rejection, of friendlessness, of rootlessness." [12]

A person's social needs, however, go beyond getting love and avoiding loneliness. Giving affection is also a very significant aspect of a person's social needs. Giving and receiving are both important. This is particularly relevant to Christian persons. For them, giving is an important way of expressing the Christian faith.

It is who we are as Christians. Christ said, "love one another; as I have loved you" (John 13:34). Paul stated, "Be devoted to one another in brotherly love" (Rom. 12:10).

There are many ways a church relates to this area of need. The church is a fellowship of believers where persons are united in the body of Christ. Many of the small-group activities of the church meet the affiliative needs of persons. The ways that we reach out to others through ministries give opportunity for expressions of love.

The need for love and acceptance is universal. Until a person has experienced some measure of fulfillment of these needs, he cannot achieve the potential that God has placed in him.

Esteem Needs

Esteem is a yet higher order of need than affiliation, safety, and physical well-being. Apparently all persons in our society have a need for a stable, firmly based, usually high evaluation of themselves, for self-respect, for self-esteem, and for the esteem of others.[13] The esteem needs can be divided into two categories: self-esteem and esteem from others.

Self-esteem includes such needs as the desire for confidence, competence, mastery, adequacy, achievement, independence, and freedom.[14] It is on a person's self-esteem that self-image is built. A person's self-image is often a controlling factor in his happiness and achievement. Psychotherapists have made much about a person "playing out his tapes" and the difficulty of intervention to change a person's preconceived tape. Also, it appears that when a person reaches his preconceived level of status or prestige, the strength of this need tends to decline and become a matter of maintenance rather than further advancement.[15]

For example, a person may be highly motivated until he reaches his perceived high-water mark in Christian development. At that point he ceases to grow because he has satisfied his self-image. A person's self-image seems to place an imaginary lid on his motivation to grow and develop.

At the same time, many persons are frustrated in their midyears because they have accomplished all of their goals (family, education, and so on) but have not arrived at their preconceived level of achievement. This is what psychologists are calling the midcareer crisis. At this point persons have to shift emotionally from tangible goals to quality of life goals. This is not an easy transition.

To have the esteem of others is the second category of esteem needs. Esteem from others includes the need for prestige, recognition, acceptance, attention, status, reputation, and appreciation.[16] Each of us wants and needs to be appreciated by others. A person's self-esteem is largely built on the feedback that is received from others. However, there is a real danger to basing one's self-esteem totally on such feedback. Feedback from others often stems from that person's needs and includes many biases. Maslow states that "the most stable and therefore most healthy self-esteem is based on deserved respect from others rather than on external fame or celebrity and unwarranted adulation." [17]

Esteem needs are intricately involved in a person's church life. Because the church and Christian leaders represent an important place in the life of a Christian, the affirmation or rejection a person receives in this arena is highly significant to his self-esteem. Rejection by a minister is for many persons like rejection by God. For this reason, ministers have the power to bless or curse.

Growth Needs

Within each person is the need to become all he can become. Maslow calls this self-actualization and believes that the need emerges only after a reasonable satisfaction of affiliation and esteem needs are met.[18]

The pursuit of a person's growth needs also appears to be different from other need areas. Physiological, safety, affiliation, and esteem needs appear to operate in a cycle. The cycle begins with a deficit or disequilibrium. Out of this need a goal is set. Behavior to reach the goal follows, and the deficit is satisfied. This cycle operates hundreds of times each day. The key word is deficit. The deficit initiates the cycle.

Growth action, on the other hand, appears to stem not from a deficit but from a need to achieve and become. In Maslow's later work he describes a whole new list of needs that he calls being-values. This list includes wholeness, perfection, completion, justice, aliveness, richness, simplicity, beauty, goodness, uniqueness, effortlessness, playfulness, truth, and self-sufficiency.[19]

David McClelland and his associates at Harvard have also done considerable study related to a person's need to achieve. Their studies show that some persons have a high need for achievement. These people tend to stretch themselves to become all their potential will allow.[20]

The apostle Paul appears to have been strongly influenced by growth needs. In Philippians 3:14 he stated, "I press toward the mark for the prize of the high calling of God in Christ Jesus." In Christian circles, the term "being on mission" is often used. This concept expresses well the concept of stretching to become all that God has given the capacity to become and directing that capacity toward the achievement of a meaningful end.

A person who is self-actualized is mission-oriented. He responds to his other needs, but he is not trapped in the deficit cycle.

These categories of needs—physiological, safety, social, esteem, and growth—represent an attempt to classify the forces that motivate the behavior of persons into a framework for study. These needs represent the pulls of life. None of these categories is more Christian than another. God made all of man. The Holy Spirit works through all aspects of man's personality. Problems arise not because man has these God-given needs but from the excesses which may develop.

Part II
What About Manipulation?

Manipulations are so much a part of our everyday life that the unskilled observer notices only the very obvious or hurtful. They are like birds which are all about us in our natural world. Most of us are fleetingly aware that the birds are there, but save for the common ones, how many of them do we actually identify or describe? [21]

—*Everett L. Shostrom*

Unit II.
What About
Manipulation?

3
Manipulator or Actualizer?

The need of persons to influence the behavior of other persons or groups of persons is universal and as old as man. Children learn at a very early age how to get their way with their parents. By the time a person reaches the teen years, he has developed and refined a whole repertoire of ways to influence others. The art isn't limited to children and teens, however. Every adult has a playbook stuffed full of tried and proven influences.

For many persons and groups, human motivation has become a science. Sales organizations study the responses of persons and seek to develop the perfect sales presentation. Advertisers test their methods carefully to insure that their clients will get a predictable reaction. Managers study organizational behavior to make certain that the highest productivity and employee morale is achieved. Oh yes! Ministers too are continually seeking to understand the factors that motivate persons to achieve and maintain a high level of Christian service.

Within itself this desire to understand ourselves and others is certainly not bad. Nor is it bad to want to influence the behavior of others. Jesus made it very clear that his mission was to influence persons. "For the son of man is come to seek and to save that which was lost" (Luke 19:10).

The real issue is control. As a leader, am I seeking to help an individual control himself toward goals which he under the Spirit's leadership finds beneficial? Or am I seeking to control him toward goals which I find beneficial? To put it another way, am I going to be an actualizer or a manipulator?

Manipulation and Actualization Defined

In his book *Man, the Manipulator,* Everett Shostrom defines a manipulator as "a person who exploits, uses, and/or controls himself and others as things in certain self-defeating ways." [22] Manipulation thus reduces persons to things and seeks to exploit them for good or evil ends.

Actualization, a term borrowed from Abraham Maslow, is the opposite of manipulation. An actualizer is a person who appreciates himself and his fellowman as persons of worth created in the image of God with unique gifts and abilities. The goal of an actualizer is to help persons discover and release their potential.

Like so many other opposite behavior patterns, few persons operate totally from only one end of the spectrum. Almost every person is both an actualizer and a manipulator. But like other behavior patterns, persons tend to lean primarily in one direction or the other. The goal of a Christian leader should be to become more actualizer and less manipulator.

A Minister's Dilemma

The actualization/manipulation question is a particularly tough problem for ministers. A minister feels heavily his concern that persons choose the best way of life. He has dedicated his life to helping others become more Christlike. He hurts deeply when he sees persons caught in the demonic web of deceit. This intense level of concern makes it all too easy to accept an "ends justifies the means" philosophy.

A leader's ego and self-esteem also come into play. While a minister honestly seeks to see and relate to persons as Christ would, he must also acknowledge and respond to his humanness. Each of us wants to succeed as a leader. We need success to feel good about ourselves and to meet the perceived expectations of others who are important to us. While manipulative leadership behavior may not be theologically acceptable, it is hard to resist temptation when our ego and self-esteem are at stake.

Thus the dilemma! Christlikeness is the most urgent need of our world. Ministers feel most keenly the desire to help persons experience the abundant life. But equally strong is the conviction concerning the value of persons and a person's God-given freedom of choice. On the one hand we strongly desire to get persons to choose Christ's way, regardless of method. But on the other hand, we dare not reduce God's creation to a mere thing through manipulative behavior.

The thesis of this book is that Christian leadership requires positive, courageous action that is characterized by actualization rather than manipulation. Jesus said, "I am come that they might have life, and that they might have it more abundantly" (John 10:10). Thus, the Magna Charta of Christian motivation—helping persons discover and experience fully the abundant life.

A Closer Look at Manipulation

A person is conditioned from a very early age to be a manipulator. In many ways his family environment teaches that success is getting what we want and making people like it. A child sees his mother and father modeling manipulation. Television also adds its effect. The child begins to experiment and sharpen his skills in his relations with family and friends.

The amount of time and energy that most persons spend concerning and playing manipulation games is staggering. In fact, we are so conditioned to manipulative behavior that only the most obvious and blatant behavior is noticed or questioned.

The church is certainly not exempt from this conditioning effect. The fact that conflict and confrontation are so opposite to our idealized view of church fellowship often promotes game playing rather than openness. Harmony is a goal that must be sought at all costs. A person's church experience can reinforce his manipulative habits and skills.

The point is that we are all involved in manipulation. Skills are developed at an early age, and the rut tends to get deeper as a person moves through life. The tragedy is that the effort we expend in manipulative growing could be used to enrich our relationship and to experience more fully the abundant life. The deeper one journeys into the wilderness of manipulation, the more stagnant and unfulfilling his life becomes. Honest, open, joyous relationships are only an elusive dream.

Types of Manipulators

Manipulators may be passive or aggressive. Although an aggressive manipulator, such as a dictator, is the type of person who epitomizes manipulation in the minds of most persons, this type of behavior is not necessarily the most powerful. In fact, when a passive manipulator and an aggressive manipulator compete, the passive player usually wins. For example, staff member "Come On Strong" has a tendency to run over staff member "Poor Me." Poor Me, a passive manipulator, baits Come On Strong to abuse and dominate him. Now Poor Me plays the classic passive game of injustice collecting and causes Come On Strong to feel loads of guilt.

An aggressive manipulator uses active, direct methods to control. He assumes a power role in a relationship. Controlling others builds his ego. This type of person usually chooses his associates very carefully. He often picks associates that he can dominate. When challenged, he tends to press harder to achieve his basic manipulative strategy such as verbal assault or threat of rejection. If this isn't successful, he may seek to discount the credibility of his challenger. As a last resort he may withdraw and pout.

A passive manipulator is much more elusive. This

person controls by being helpless. He allows the aggressive manipulator to control him. By his passiveness the aggressor goes out on a limb and saws it off behind him. He wins by losing. The passive manipulator is not predictable. He wields a whole repertoire of passive approaches. For example, a person who controls by being Mr. Nice Guy may shift to the weakling if he is attacked by a bully. The passive manipulator usually picks his strategy based on the approach of the aggressor.

Why Manipulation?

If manipulative behavior is so common, why? The root problem is self-esteem, but this expresses itself in several ways.

Power is at the head of the list. Many persons need power to prove their self-worth. The prize of the manipulation may not be the result. The act of winning is often the real prize.

An inability to love is another causal factor. A person who does not appreciate himself is constantly trying to prove his worth. The ability to manipulate himself or others becomes a temporary balm for lagging appreciation of self and others.

Fear of failure is another facet of the problem. Failure is a bitter pill to swallow, particularly if a person has experienced several unsuccessful ventures. The person begins to doubt his self-worth. The fear of another failure can cause a person to justify almost any behavior pattern.

Fear of being vulnerable is another symptom. "Play

it close to the vest." "Protect yourself at all costs." These are the guiding principles of a person who is afraid to expose his humanness. Through manipulation he protects his insecurity.

The message is clear. A person who does not have a sense of self-worth will find it very difficult to rise above manipulative patterns of behavior. Because few persons are not plagued with insecurity in some areas, the road to more actualizing behavior must include a continuing examination of who we are and the environment in which we live.

Responding to Manipulative Games

Eric Berne's book *Games People Play* has made popular the concept of interpersonal contests in which people seek to achieve their goals. Many of the games people play are manipulative. To some extent we are all manipulators and live in a world of manipulation. Thus, we have no choice but to respond to manipulation in some way. The way a person responds to manipulative games is a true test of his Christian ethic and character.

The basic strategy of dealing with manipulative behavior is to not play the game. If a person chooses to compete with the manipulator, the game continues to escalate until someone wins. A skilled manipulator is very deceptive. He will play his game as cleverly as a good chess player. He calculates his opponents' moves and cuts off his escape before he makes his move.

A person must not only commit himself not to take

the bait of a manipulator but also learn to anticipate the behavior—see it coming. Otherwise, the manipulator will have the trap set before the unsuspecting victim realizes the game is in progress. As the next chapter explains, some of the games are very common and recognizable.

A third general principle relates to the worth of persons. Manipulation is a destructive behavior. It is easy to "write off" a manipulative person. Obviously, a Christian leader should resist this temptation. Although an attitude of forgiveness is sometimes hard to muster, all persons are created by God and valued by him.

More specifically, there are four basic approaches that can be used to respond to manipulative behavior: (1) counterattack, (2) withdraw, (3) patronize, and (4) actualize.

Counterattack

The counterattack is a very common response. This is a defensive reaction to the manipulator. The response can be passive or aggressive. In effect, the counterattack is responding with another manipulative act.

The People's Voice: "Brother Frank, I sure hope you will change your mind about trying this new grading system for Sunday School. A number of people have called me and they are very upset about the proposed changes."

Aggressive Response: "Just how many people have talked with you? I want their names, too."

Passive Response: "This hurts me that you would bring

this kind of message. I'm doing the best I can to develop an effective Bible study program."

The aggressive counterattack is a frontal attack on the other person. Open hostility is the likely result. This response happens most often when a person loses his temper. From a leader's point of view, it can be justified if he is trying to force the action and is willing to run the risk of open conflict.

A passive counterattack also brings hostility, but it goes underground and usually does not erupt openly. The hostility is passed around behind the scenes. In the long run the destructive results may be greater.

Problems are seldom solved through counterattack. This approach injects an extra emotional issue into the conversation. The real issue is pushed aside for the two parties to enter an emotional power struggle.

Withdraw

Withdrawal is another way to respond to manipulation. This response may appear to be the easy way out. One method of withdrawal is to be silent and communicate nonverbally. The nonverbal signal, however, may be a counterattack as well as a withdrawal. Another method of withdrawal is to change the subject. A third type of withdrawal is a peace-at-any-cost attitude, even if it means to acquiesce.

Influence Peddler: "Preacher, I can go with you on that Family Life Center if you'll help me get the church to pave that back parking lot."

No Response: "Thanks, Jim."
Change the Subject: "Speaking of parking, did you notice the way the Broadway Church had resurfaced their main lot?"
Peace at Any Cost: "We do need more parking. I'll see what I can do."

On the surface the withdrawal response to manipulation appears not to be destructive. This is true if short-term peace and calm are the principal goals of the relationship. Withdrawal, however, is an avoidance strategy. Sooner or later the issues must be met.

Patronize

To patronize another person means to be condescending toward him. A patronizing response to manipulation is disallowing the other person's feelings. You may say, "That's good enough for the manipulator. He deserves what he gets." However, patronizing another person is belittling that person. Also, it can cut off further communication with the person.

The Injustice Collector: "Pastor, I have talked with my youth about not standing in the halls during Sunday School, but I can't get them to listen to me. You probably don't have time to talk to me either."
Pastor: "You shouldn't feel that way. I'm sure they really hear you. One of these days they'll surprise you."
Or: "Sure people listen to you."
Or: "Try again. I'll bet you'll find them more receptive next time."

Again, nothing is really being solved. The individual has not been helped. Patronizing a neurotic person will only bring him back for more. A more healthy person will get the message that you really do not think of him as a person of worth, even if he is a manipulator.

Confront

To confront means to deal with a manipulative person in an honest and open way. An actualizer does not take the manipulative bait. He speaks the truth in love. A confronter uses exploration, involvement, evaluation, and negotiation to confront and diffuse the act of manipulation.

The Calculator: "Brother Jim, the facts are very plain to me. This purchase will wreck the financial stability of our program."
Confronter: "Let me hear your findings. You may have some facts the committee has not considered."
Or: "I can see you feel strongly about this purchase. I'll get a copy of the committee data for you. I'd like for you to compare your facts with theirs."
Or: "What do you feel are the major weaknesses and strengths of the proposal? Here are a couple of strengths I'd like to add to yours. It appears to me that the committee has a pretty strong case."

The confronter uses probing questions and avoids emotionally loaded statements. He affirms and shows appreciation for the other person. He stands firm on his convictions but allows others to disagree without feeling put down. Getting things out in the open in an adult way is very important. Only then can the issue be dealt with creatively. The other three response patterns—counterattack, withdraw, and patronize—only tend to create open hostility or send feelings underground.

This chapter has dealt with the theory of manipulation and actualization. The next chapter will explore some specific manipulative games. All persons are manipulators to some extent. Hopefully, these chapters will help you recognize and deal with these shortcomings in your own behavior as well as those to whom you relate.

4
Some Manipulators I've Known

Manipulation is a game of many plays that can be run from a wide variety of formations. Every minister is aware of some or all of these plays. We all use these plays and defend against them. Perhaps this discussion will increase our awareness of the self-defeating nature of the various games, whether on the offense or defense.

The Influence Peddler

Basic Approach: "I'll scratch your back if you'll scratch mine when I give the signal."

This is the classic game of influence peddling. The manipulator makes it clear that his support for your program is dependent on favors that you may do for him now or in the future. This is a very familiar game to a minister. A power person in the congregation says, "Preacher, I can go with you on building that recreation building if you'll help me get the lot on the back corner included in the package. What we really need around here is more parking space."

Or an organization leader says, "Brother Frank, the extra fifteen minutes in Sunday School sounds OK to me, but I'm counting on you to hold the line on the

THE INFLUENCE PEDDLER

Basic Approach

"I'll scratch your back if you'll scratch mine."

Strategies

1. Be direct but attack the problem, not the person.
2. Build your case on facts that collaborate with his.
3. Avoid the need to reach consensus at all costs.
4. Keep the commitment you make.

Wednesday night schedule."

Analysis: This manipulator knows the meaning of power. He has probably developed his power base by trading favors. Because this person has come straight across with his offer, you can be equally direct in your response. This type of person appreciates directness if you do not threaten to control him or take away his power. He tends to distrust persons who are subtle and indirect. The basic strategy of dealing with the influence peddler is to: (1) be direct but attack the problem, not the person; (2) build your case on facts that are compatible with his; (3) avoid the need to reach consensus at all costs; (4) keep the commitment you make. You may use statements like:

- The issue is the Sunday morning schedule. I need your input on that, but I'm not ready to discuss the Wednesday schedule.
- Let's compare your facts and mine.
- I hope you will be in the meeting Monday evening; we will need to hear your proposal.
- You can count on me to present your ideas and feelings as accurately as I can.

Avoid statements like:

- If you had studied this issue as much as I have, you wouldn't feel that way.
- You are ethically and morally wrong to make such a statement.
- I resent your trying to pressure me.
- I'll work behind the scenes to support your position, but please don't bring this up in the meeting.

THE PEOPLE'S CHOICE

Basic Approach

"A number of people have talked to me and they say . . ."

Strategies

1. Try not to be defensive.
2. Help the person evaluate the data he is sharing.
3. Involve the person in appropriate responsible action to resolve the issue.

The People's Choice

Basic Approach: "A number of people have talked to me and they say . . ."

This manipulator sees himself as the voice of the people. His basic strategy is to win through intimidation. He implies, "You wouldn't want to risk turning the people against your leadership, would you?" Of course, you can't find out who "they" are. He must protect the confidentiality of his sources.

Analysis: The person using this game is usually of the same opinion as the persons he is quoting. In fact, in many cases he may have initiated the conversation with the other persons. He may lack the courage to present his case in a more direct way. He is probably not sure of your reaction. Perhaps in the past you have tended to react aggressively. This indirect method gives him protection and offers a quick exit. The basic strategy of dealing with this manipulator is to: (1) try not to be defensive, (2) help the person evaluate the data he is sharing, and (3) involve the person in appropriate responsible action to resolve the issue. You may use statements like:

- Thank you for sharing with me.
- Why do you think these people feel this way?
- What action do you think we should take?
- I need your help in resolving this.

Avoid statements like:

- I think you missed what they said.
- Just how many people have really talked with you?

THE WEAKLING

Basic Approach

"You wouldn't hurt me, would you?"

Strategies

1. Assure the person that you are concerned about his welfare.
2. Share some of your own feelings about the issue.
3. Assure the person that after a decision is made you will try to help him cope with it.
4. Do not feel guilty.

- Are you sure you are not the only person who feels this way?
- I've been aware of this for a long time. I don't think it's anything to worry about.
- You tell these people that if they have anything to say they can say it to me!

The Weakling

Basic Approach: "You wouldn't hurt me, would you?"

In this passive play, the manipulator appeals to your sense of fair play. His theme is "surely you wouldn't kick a person when he's down." He implies that possibly you could not deal with the guilt you would feel if you abused him. This game is not limited to persons in the congregation. Some ministers use this play deftly.

Analysis: The weakling is usually baiting you to be overly aggressive. Only if you play his game will his strategy work. Remember, he wins by losing. The basic strategy is to: (1) assure the person that you are concerned about his welfare, (2) share some of your own feelings about the issue, (3) assure the person that after the decision is made you will try to help him cope with it, and (4) do not feel guilty. You may use statements like:

- How can I help you?
- You can count on me to be your friend.
- I believe the pros and cons of this issue are . . .
- Regardless of the decision I'll be your friend.

Avoid statements like:

- If you'll get out of the way, I can get this done.
- You shouldn't feel that way.

THE CALCULATOR

Basic Approach

"The facts are very plain to me."

Strategies

1. Avoid a direct attack on this person's technical conclusion.
2. Affirm his technical competence.
3. Help him see that decisions are based on feelings as well as facts.
4. Let him participate in but not control the decision-making process.

- Nobody's going to hurt you.
- This is a cruel world, isn't it?

The Calculator

Basic Approach: "The facts are very plain to me."

This is another aggressive intimidation play. The manipulator implies that it would be very stupid to interpret the facts in any way other than the way he sees them. He implies that the minister would be risking the loss of the confidence of the thinking people in his congregation. He is appealing to a person's need to think of himself as a wise person.

Analysis: This manipulator needs reinforcement of his technical competence. Technical skills are likely the stack poles for his ego structure. Thus, he leads with his strength. He assumes that you too view technical competence as very important and that you would avoid embarrassment at any cost. The basic strategy is to: (1) avoid a direct attack on this person's technical conclusion, (2) affirm his technical competence, (3) help him to see that decisions are based on feelings as well as facts, (4) let him participate in but not control the decision-making process. You may use statements like:

- Please interpret the situation to me.
- What do you see as the major strengths and weaknesses of this program?
- I can see that you feel strongly about this issue. I've sensed that feelings are as important as facts in this case.
- Will you go with me to the next committee meeting to present these findings?

THE OMNIPOTENT FATHER

Basic Approach

"If you had only listened to me" or "I could have told you that would happen."

Strategies

1. Stay calm and try not to be defensive.
2. Be a good listener.
3. Don't make promises that you can't keep.
4. Share other ideas and ask for advice in advance.

- Have you compared your data with the committee's report?

Statements to avoid:

- Your facts seem illogical to me.
- I'm sorry, but your sources are not up-to-date.
- I don't have time to talk about your idea. (If you don't, set a date.)
- I wish you didn't feel this way.

The Omnipotent Father

Basic Approach: "If you had only listened to me" or "I could have told you that would happen."

The manipulator is trying to bring the person back into line. This is the favorite play used by a manipulator after a person has broken from his manipulative grasp. The manipulator implies, "You don't really want to risk failure again, do you? If you'll listen to the omnipotent father, I'll take care of you."

Analysis: This manipulator is threatened by the fact that he may be losing or has never had control of your behavior. He needs to be seen as a person of great wisdom and influence. His method makes you doubt your sufficiency. Some persons would desire to make you dependent on their approval. Other persons simply want to be a confidant of the leader. The basic strategy of dealing with this manipulator is to: (1) stay calm and try not to be defensive, (2) be a good listener, (3) don't make promises that you can't keep. Use statements like:

- It would have been good to have had that information before I made the decision.

THE DIVINE MESSENGER

Basic Approach

"I've received a special revelation from God."

Strategies

1. Affirm his relationship to God and your case for him as a person.
2. Affirm your own relationship to God.
3. Help the person understand that two persons may view God's will differently.
4. Help the person evaluate his feelings.

- Help me evaluate the strengths and weaknesses of the plan.
- In the future, feel free to share this kind of data with me.
- I appreciate your insight and help.

Avoid statements like:

- Why didn't you help me when I needed you?
- I'll always check with you in the future before we launch a new program.
- I know I make lots of mistakes, but I do the best I can.

The Divine Messenger

Basic Approach: "I've received a special revelation from God."

This type of manipulation is the ultimate threat of rejection. To go against this person's ideas is to go against God. There is a vast difference between being spiritually sensitive to God's leadership and using God to put others down. As God's children, Christians have a special relationship to him. But persons sometimes project their will as God's will. This is presuming on God. God rejects sin, but not persons. Parenthetically, this play is not limited to church members.

Analysis: This type of manipulator wants to state his case in such a way that no one dares try to refute it. In reality, this person is not too sure of himself. He wants to avoid a rational debate on the issue. Thus he goes to the highest source of credibility. The basic strategy of dealing with the manipulator is to: (1) affirm his relationship to God and your care for him as a

THE
MARTYR

Basic Approach

"Look what I've given up for the church."

Strategies

1. Don't play his game.
2. Help the person explore his feelings.
3. Assure the person that you care for him.
4. Don't feel guilty.

person, and (2) affirm your own relationship to God. Use statements like:

- It's good that you are sensitive to God's leadership.
- I feel good about the insight God is giving me regarding this issue.
- Tell me about your insight in the matter.
- Could God be leading us in different directions?

Avoid statements like:

- You're just too pious.
- God gives us minds to think with.
- Don't pull that God thing on me!
- Whatever you say.

The Martyr

Basic Approach: "Look what I've given up for the church."

This is the classical martyr play. The manipulator seeks to get persons to feel guilty because they have caused the manipulator to not get what is due him from life. This game is often played to obtain a desired response from a person or group. The manipulator may claim to have given up fortune, fame, or great experiences.

Analysis: A martyr needs someone to take responsibility for his unhappiness. He chose to be the person he is, but he is unhappy with the outcome. He feels trapped. Since he feels a loss of control of his own life, he seeks to regain a bit of self-esteem through controlling another person. In desperation he reaches out to get others to bear the guilt for his plight. If he suc-

THE INJUSTICE COLLECTOR

Basic Approach

"No one ever listens to me."

Strategies

1. Learn to spot the injustice collector before you have taken the bait.
2. Demonstrate genuine affirmation for the person.
3. Give the person an opportunity to input ideas.
4. Don't feel guilty.

ceeds, he achieves a measure of satisfaction. His success will probably launch him into a continuous pattern of playing the martyr. The basic strategy of dealing with this person is to not play his game—to not assume responsibility for his actions. You may say:

- I'm sorry, but I can't assume responsibility for your feelings.
- What can I do to help you deal with your feelings of despair?

Avoid statements like:

- I've given up quite a lot myself.
- I wish you wouldn't talk like that.
- That's too bad; I'm so sorry for you.

The Injustice Collector

Basic Approach: "No one ever listens to me."

This is the passive play of an injustice collector. He has been abused by the whole world. How could anyone possibly add one more ounce of injustice on this person's back? This person has the capacity to heap great loads of guilt upon another person. Most often an injustice collector is suffering from an acute identity crisis and is experiencing mild paranoia.

Analysis: The self-esteem of an injustice collector has reached rock bottom. He does not have the stamina to be an aggressive manipulator. He has learned that he can win by losing. He can bring down the "big game" with the skillful way he heaps guilt on an aggressive person. The basic strategy of dealing with this person is to: (1) learn to spot an injustice collector before you have taken the bait, (2) demonstrate genuine affirmation

THE CRITICAL PARENT

Basic Approach

"No self-respecting person would dare give less than his best."

Strategies

1. Refuse to assume the child role.
2. Give adult responses to his communication.
3. Let the person know that you will be responsible for your action or lack of it.

for him as a person, and (3) give him an opportunity to input his ideas. You can use statements like:

- I would like to hear your ideas on that subject.
- Tell me more about your feelings.
- Thanks, your input will be heard.

Avoid statements like:

- Sure, people listen to you.
- I don't blame them, the way you complain all the time.
- Don't tell me about your problems.

The Critical Parent

Basic Approach: "No self-respecting person would dare give less than his best."

This manipulative game seeks to shame a person into a desired response. Implied is a threat of rejection. In fact, this play even suggests that a person should reject himself as a person of worth. Regardless of the motive behind the play, the result is the same. The person using the play is seeking to control the person or group of persons.

Analysis: The omnipotent parent has built his ego structure around feeling that he is aloof from the muck and mire of life. He sees himself as a person of great wisdom. He reinforces his ego by telling others what is best for them. When persons appear to not measure up to his expectations, he can quickly become a judge and sentence them to shame for their imperfection. He needs to manipulate persons to maintain his self-concept of being able to pull strings and get things done.

The basic strategy for dealing with this person is

THE VOICE OF EXPERIENCE

Basic Approach

"Someday you'll be able to understand what we are discussing."

Strategies

1. Do not be intimidated by his rules and regulations.
2. Be a quick learner.
3. Quietly make your input into the vocabulary.
4. Don't push. Look for the right time to make a significant contribution.

to: (1) refuse to assume a child role, (2) give adult responses to his communication, and (3) let him know that you will be responsible for your action or lack of it. You might use statements like:

- This job is important. It deserves our best.
- I feel good about my decision regarding this project.
- What kind of expectations do you have regarding this project?

Avoid statements like:

- What I do is none of your business.
- I will feel terrible if I can't get the job done.
- I'll do my best not to disappoint you.

The Voice of Experience

Basic Approach: "Someday you'll be able to understand what we are discussing."

This is a very subtle form of manipulation. Persons are put in a rookie class and denied input into decision making because the initiated have a special vocabulary. Through an exclusive glossary the manipulator reinforces the pecking order. A strong need to belong can cause a person to endure numerous manipulations with the hope of being accepted. Economic status, education, and social status can also be used in the same way.

Analysis: The chairman of the board builds his self-esteem around some prized possession. It gives him a feeling of status. He guards it proudly. Before others can share in this exclusive fellowship, they must pass his test. He is able to maintain his top dog position because he can control the initiation rites. The basic strategy of dealing with this manipulator is to: (1) not be intimidated by his rules and regulations, (2) be a quick learner, and (3) quietly make your input into the vocabulary. Use statements like:

- I need your help to understand the way this group functions.
- Could you define that term for me?
- To be helpful in this discussion, I need a brief orientation.

Avoid statements like:

- This is the most ridiculous word game I've ever seen.
- I'll not try to participate until I feel comfortable.

These are but ten of the more prevalent manipulative plays. They are certainly not the exclusive property of either lay persons or ministers. Since each of us is part manipulator, these games are not only intended to help ministers confront manipulative persons but to also help ministers examine their behavior.

Part III
Now About Motivation

"And my God shall supply all your needs according to His riches in glory in Christ Jesus" (Phil. 4:19, NASB).

Physical Needs

"For this reason I say to you, do not be anxious for your life, as to what you shall eat, or what you shall drink; nor for your body, as to what you shall put on. Is not life more than food, and the body than clothing? Look at the birds of the air, that they do not sow, neither do they reap, nor gather into barns, and yet your heavenly Father feeds them. Are you not worth much more than they?" (Matt. 6:25-26, NASB).

Safety Needs

"Let not your heart be troubled; believe in God, believe also in Me. In My Father's house are many dwelling places; if it were not so, I would have told you; for I go to prepare a place for you. And if I go and prepare a place for you, I will come again, and receive you to Myself; that where I am, there you may be also" (John 14:1-3, NASB).

Belonging Needs

"Behold, I stand at the door and knock; if any one hears My voice and opens the door, I will come in to Him, and will dine with him, and he with Me" (Rev. 3:20, NASB).

Self-Esteem Needs

"But thanks be to God, who always leads us in His triumph in Christ, and manifests through us the sweet aroma of the knowledge of Him in every place" (2 Cor. 2:14, NASB).

Self-Actualization Needs

"You did not choose Me, but I chose you, and appointed you, that you should go and bear fruit, and that your fruit should remain, that whatever you ask of the Father in My name, He may give to you" (John 15:16, NASB).

5
The Basic Principles

Successful leadership is certainly more than just controlling the desire to manipulate others and dealing effectively with manipulative persons. Manipulation is the negative side of being an influencer. Actualization is the positive side of the issue. All persons are motivated. An actualizer seeks to help persons to be positively motivated toward a worthy goal. The remainder of this book will seek to explore the positive side of influencing the behavior of self and others—that is, why persons are motivated, how persons are motivated, and the keys to building a climate that will help persons become and continue to be motivated. The focus will be on Christian service. However, the concepts may be applied to family and occupational relationships.

The Principles of Motivation

A statement of certain principles will serve as a launching point for the exploration of motivation. These concepts are foundational to the remaining chapters.

Triggered from Within

Several years ago I was asked to present a paper on motivation as part of a denominational convocation.

The paper began with the statement, "It is impossible for one person to motivate another person." I'll not soon forget the fire in the eyes of the participants because they found this statement offensive. They had devoted much of their ministry to motivating others. Who was I to say they had not motivated and could not motivate another person?

That's just the issue. All too often ministers approach motivation as something a leader does. This concept makes one person responsible for the behavior of another. On the contrary, each of us is responsible for and accountable to God for our own behavior. Motivation is something that stems from within each individual. This is good theology. God has given each person the freedom of choice. The Scriptures say, "Keep thy heart with all diligence; for out of it are the issues of life" (Prov. 4:23) and "For as he thinketh in his heart, so is he" (Prov. 23:7).

This is the most basic of all principles of motivation— motivation is a personal matter that is decided by each person for himself. This is not to say that a leader cannot influence the behavior of persons. Certainly he can offer incentives that influence persons to act. These incentives often take the form of a carrot—reward— or a stick—punishment. Also, there are other types of external stimuli in the environment, such as temperature, that affect a person's motivation.

Admittedly, to say that a leader cannot motivate another person but that he can influence his behavior with incentives is a technicality. However, it is an important technicality for two reasons. First, the principle of self-motivation makes each person responsible for his actions, not the leader. Second, this principle implies that the leader's basic responsibility is not to motivate persons but to build a climate in which they will become motivated. This is entirely consistent with equipping functions of ministry discussed by Paul in Ephesians 4.

External incentives are no better than their value to the person to whom they are being offered. The leader who seeks to lead by carrot and stick methods must spend much of his time trying to find bigger and more appealing carrots and effective sticks.

Think of the persons you know who maintain a high level of Christian motivation. Is their motivation primarily triggered by things that a leader does? I doubt it. These persons respond to leadership, but their basic motivation is sustained from within their own being.

Based on Needs

If a person's motivation is triggered from within himself, what are the triggers that cause him to respond? His needs! God made us that way. When I first began to study motivation, I tried to separate physical, social, and spiritual motivation. It was a great moment for me when I accepted the fact that God relates to me through all areas of my life. God is not limited to those needs in my life that relate to helping others and loving him. He made me in his own image. A person has the freedom to feel and respond to the Spirit's leadership in all of life's stimuli. By the same token, a person also has the freedom to respond to the wooing of Satan.

Needs come in all shapes, sizes, and intensities. Some needs are primary and innate—the needs for food, water, elimination, a comfortable temperature, and so on. Primary needs are those physiological needs that keep a person alive. Other needs are secondary and acquired. These acquired needs are social and achievement needs.

Scientists disagree concerning the source of motivation, but most agree that motivation is a cyclical process that begins with a need and ends with satisfaction. Figure 1 illustrates the process. It begins with a need or deficit. Feeling the need(s), a person sets a goal to meet the need(s). Appropriate action is taken to achieve the goal. When the goal is achieved, the need is satisfied. When the need recurs, the process is repeated.

Here is an example. John has a need for his ego to be bolstered. He sets a goal to get recognition that will stroke his ego. He works hard to present an excellent community analysis to the church. The church rewards him by accepting his report and voting to begin several new ministries. John feels good. His ego has been strengthened. John's ego need may not be the only need that causes him to work hard on the project, but it is one important factor.

Although the process of motivation is primarily deficit-oriented, Abraham Maslow also identified a process he called growth motivation. In this process the need appears to never be satisfied. Like the North Star or the pot of gold at the end of the rainbow, it seems to continually move ahead as a person progresses toward it. This need for growth is often associated with a cause or mission in life. Paul expressed this process of motivation when he stated: "I press toward the goal for the prize of the upward call of God in Christ Jesus" (Phil. 3:14, NASB).

The payoff for growth motivation is the pursuit of the goal itself and the progress that is being made. Complete satisfaction is never reached. Maslow's research revealed that few persons expend a significant amount of their motivational energies in pursuit of growth needs.

Blocking of goal achievement is another reality that should be noted. Blocking occurs when a person is prevented in some way from acting to reach a goal and satisfy a need. When goal achievement is blocked, a person will either intensify his behavior, establish the goal, suppress the need, or choose a new strategy. For example, a person who has set a goal to meet a belonging need by joining a Bible study class may be rejected by the group. This person may try harder to get group acceptance and be rejected even more soundly. Or he may set a goal to join another group. If he suppresses the need, he may become self-depreciating. Leaders should be sensitive to blockage. Abnormal behavior is the likely result of a blocked goal.

From Multiple Stimuli

A third foundational concept relates to the multiple, simultaneous stimuli. A person's behavior is seldom a response to a single need. It is very difficult for a person to pinpoint one single need as the source of a particular behavior. Even the act of eating is often tied

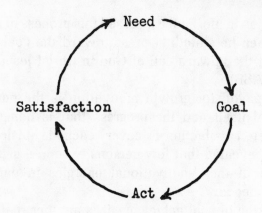

Deficit Process

The Processes of Motivation

Figure 1

Growth Process

to several needs. For example, it is an accepted fact that eating can relate to the physical needs, social needs, and the self-esteem needs.

In the Christian service realm, do persons accept teaching positions just because of their love for God and their desire to serve him? Not many. Most persons also are responding to the ego and the need to belong. This is not bad. It is just a fact. Remember, if we let him, God can work through all our needs.

Variations in Potency

A fourth foundational concept relates to the relative potency of needs. Some needs generally are more potent than others. Also, potency of a particular need can vary according to the situation. Abraham Maslow made a significant contribution to motivational theory by developing a hierarchy of needs according to their relative potency. He first classified needs in five categories: physiological, safety or security, belonging or love, self-esteem or ego, and self-actualization.[23] In a later study he refined his theory to include what he called meta needs. But for this discussion his original work is sufficient.

Figure 2 illustrates Maslow's hierarchy. His theory states that the relative potency of human needs moves from strongest potency at the base of the pyramid to the least potency at the top. Therefore, while the need for self-actualization produces the highest quality of motivation, it apparently gets the least attention because it must compete with the more basic needs.

This is a very important principle for Christian leaders. A leader may spend much of his energy seeking to relate to persons on the basis of self-actualization when they are entangled in a web of more basic needs. In the same way a leader may invest all of his efforts in building a climate based on a person's need for security and belonging. By so doing, he fails to help persons move out of the morass of these basic needs to experience the higher quality of fulfillment related to self-esteem and self-actualization.

Another facet of this principle relates to met and unmet needs. A satisfied need is not a motivator. A person who has just eaten is not motivated by food. A person whose ego needs are met does not need more affirmation—at least for a short period. A person who has a sense of belonging has more freedom to pursue ego goals that require risk.

Motivation comes from within. It stems from a variety of needs—some stronger than others. A person can let the Holy Spirit work through his needs or close him out. A Christian leader's role is to build a climate in

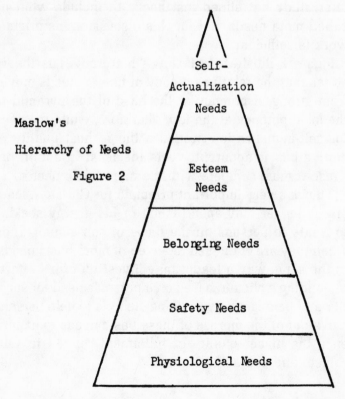

Maslow's
Hierarchy of Needs
Figure 2

which a person can fulfill his needs in a way that brings joy and wholeness.

Four Keys to Effective Motivation

Building a climate in which persons can build and sustain motivation is the goal of every leader. Thus leaders are enablers and equippers. There appear to be at least four keys to effective climate building: stability, teamwork, affirmation, and challenge. (See Figure 3.) If these conditions exist in an enterprise, motivation will occur. The leader does not perform all these actions, but he seeks to see that the climate is created. Also, balance is needed. Although some persons have greater needs in certain areas, every person needs to experience stability, teamwork, affirmation, and challenge. In the next few paragraphs each of these concepts will be introduced. Each will be discussed fully in the following chapters.

Stability

Stability relates to a person's need for safety and security. Stability helps persons accept change. It provides a climate of order, predictability, freedom from chaos, and protection. When persons feel insecure, they pull back into their shell. They lose their capacity to risk. Protection of what the person has becomes permanent. Stability is the foundation stone for a climate of motivation. Without stability the whole structure will likely crumble. Leaders who have the ability to create a climate of stability and order have discovered the first key to effective motivation.

Teamwork

A climate of teamwork relates to the need to belong and be loved. Persons need the togetherness and feeling of worth that can come from being accepted as part of a team. Certainly all teams are not created and led by the minister of a church. A Sunday School class and a training group are teams. A team relationship enables a person to receive and give affection. Both are important social needs. Leaders who establish and equip teams to operate have discovered the second key to effective motivation.

Affirmation

A climate of affirmation relates to a person's need for self-esteem. This part of the motivational climate is important because persons build their self-esteem primarily on the signals they receive from others. If a person gets good feedback from others, he tends to feel good about himself. The feedback can be in the form of criticism, however. Although a person needs to get feedback about what's right with him, he also needs honest input relating to problem areas. The difficulty is that so many people get no feedback at all. Leaders who set the example by being ministers of affirmation go a long way toward providing this needed climate in a church family.

Challenge

The climate would not be complete without challenge. Challenge relates to a person's need for purpose, meaning, and achievement. Challenge relates to being on mission. Challenge is a growth motivation process.

Key 1

STABILITY
Climate: order, predicta-
bility, freedom from chaos,
protection

Key 2

TEAMWORK
Climate: belonging, giving,
and receiving love, acceptance, interaction, togetherness

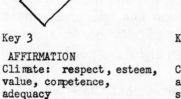

BUILDING
A CLIMATE
FOR
MOTIVATION

PRAYER   PRAYER   PRAYER   PRAYER

Key 3

AFFIRMATION
Climate: respect, esteem,
value, competence,
adequacy

Key 4

CHALLENGE
Climate: purpose, meaning,
achievement, fulfillment,
success

FOUR KEYS TO EFFECTIVE MOTIVATION

Figure 3

Without challenge the environment may lack the spark to set the enterprise on fire. Stability, teamwork, and affirmation provide the nurture that persons need to be motivated; but challenge provides the dynamic. Visionary leaders who can verbalize the mission and lead with confidence provide a stimulating climate for motivation.

The Christian's Extra Dimension

To this point, the principles and keys discussed relate equally to Christians and non-Christians. But it is time to state emphatically that the Christian experience adds an extra dimension to a person's motivation. This dimension is the power of the Holy Spirit that operates in the life of a Christian. When a person becomes a Christian, the Holy Spirit dwells in that person and becomes his helper. The Holy Spirit does not change the process of motivation. Persons continue to be motivated on the basis of needs. The Holy Spirit works through those needs to add to the quality of a person's motivation.

Because persons are need-seeking organisms, we tend to operate in our own little circles and give priority to meeting our own needs. The indwelling of the Holy Spirit enables us to transcend this self-centeredness. As a Christian, a person has the capacity for security, love, esteem, and mission that he did not have prior to accepting Christ.

It should be noted, however, that Christ saves us in our humanness, not from our humanness. Each person still has the freedom of choice. He can choose to limit the Spirit's work and miss at least part of the extra dimension of motivation that is available.

6
Key No. 1:
Stability

This chapter begins a series of chapters dealing with keys for building a climate in which persons can build a high level of motivation.

Key No. 1: Persons are more highly motivated in an environment that has order, predictability, structure, and stability.

This key relates primarily to a person's safety needs. However, as will be shown later, there is a close correlation with affiliation and esteem needs. A person's safety or security needs can be viewed from two perspectives. While the need for physical safety is the more obvious perspective, the need for emotional safety is more relevant to a person's church experiences.

Churches are giving an increasing amount of attention to the physical safety needs of persons. For years, parking lots and hallways have been well lighted; and facilities and equipment have been maintained to give adequate safety. However, with the rise in street crime, more stringent measures are being taken in many areas. Some churches are only opening certain doors with ushers trained to detect and screen dangerous persons. Parking-lot patrols are being set up to protect persons and property. Fences are being placed around areas where children play. Schedules for services and visitation are being altered to allow for greater personal security.

While the provision for physical safety is necessary in many areas, the major thrust of this chapter relates to building a climate for emotional safety and security. A person whose emotional security is threatened will react in one of three ways: fight, withdraw in fear, or become apathetic. None of these reactions produces a good climate for motivation.

Although other culprits may be involved, change and the threat of change appear to be the major harbingers of emotional insecurity in a church situation.

Understanding Change

Change occurs when the nature of a situation is altered in any way. Change can be very observable, or it can be very subtle. A change in the furniture of a classroom or worship center is very obvious. Changes in attitudes or values are more difficult to detect. Persons usually are more open with their feelings about observable changes because they know where the enemy is. Feelings about subtle changes often go underground and are much more difficult for a leader to deal with. Trying to hide change can often cause more resistance than putting the item openly on the table.

While it is true that persons often resist change, this is not always the case. Generally speaking, there is a natural preference for the familiar. Persons also find it difficult to unlearn habits that are well established.

But change often helps the enterprise and the people. The attitude of persons about change usually depends upon whether a person perceives the change to help or to hurt him. If he is helped, he is for it. If he is hurt, he is against it. Thus, when a leader is considering a change, he should calculate the number and power of the persons who will be helped and hurt. Obviously, the change should be designed as a win/win situation.

When resistance is encountered, it tends to come from a combination of several effects. People often resist change because it brings an unfamiliar environment. Just the unknown causes insecurity. The familiar is comfortable and predictable. It takes less energy to cope with a familiar situation.

A change in teachers' materials for Sunday School illustrates the point. Word came from several sources that the teachers in the Youth Division felt that the new material did not include enough Bible material. This was disturbing because an evaluation of the material showed that it did.

A training session was scheduled with a special consultant to discuss the problem. It became quickly apparent that the Bible helps were not the problem at all. The problem focused in the new format of the helps.

The teachers were very familiar with the old format and felt very uncomfortable with the new. Oddly enough, they knew of their discomfort but did not realize specifically what was causing it until the consultant helped them isolate it.

This is often the case. What a person is able to verbalize may not be the change that is causing the problem. He may just pick up a slogan that sounds good because he is not able to isolate the real cause of his frustration. In the case of the Sunday School teachers, they picked up a phrase that they knew would get the serious attention of their minister.

Resistance to change may also come because of the effect on the power structure. Almost every person in a group has a certain amount of organizational or personal power. Change will likely alter that power in some way. This is particularly threatening because a person's self-image is at stake. If a person perceives himself to be a chief, it will be hard for him to become an Indian. This is not implying that all people are power hungry, but they do want and like the power they have. For example, a person who is secretary of a class may not have any aspiration to become president, but he certainly does not want to be dislodged from the secretary job. A wise leader will carefully study the power situation as he designs planned change.

Leadership Style and Change

A minister's leadership is a crucial factor in helping persons remain motivated in the face of change. A leader is responsible for helping persons develop appropriate behavior in the new environment so that they can continue to be creative and productive. Some leaders can help a person or a group move through change with relative ease, while others have difficulty with the process. It is a matter of leadership skill and style.

A leader who is a good change facilitator has the following traits:

1. He cares about people and engenders their trust. People want a leader they can trust. It helps them feel secure. Nothing is more disconcerting to a group than to be betrayed by their leader. People must sense that a leader is helping them meet their goals—that he is concerned about them. A leader who seeks to use people to meet his own needs is soon found out.

2. He exudes confidence. A leader should have confidence in what he is doing. This is not to say that he must lie to people. Telling the truth builds trust and confidence. But when a leader puts his hand to the plow, he should not look back. People can gain security by vicariously sharing the confidence of their leader.

3. He displays enthusiasm. Humans are emotional beings. They want and need to be part of exciting ventures. A leader must have and share excitement about the enterprise. He does not have to be a "holler guy"; but in whatever way is natural to him, he must display enthusiasm.

4. He is knowledgeable. People expect a leader to do his homework. This is one way a leader gains the respect and trust of people. While it is true that some people will follow a leader because of his charisma, there are usually enough people in any group who expect good data to make this principle important. Working from good data will extend significantly the "life span" of a leader. A leader who senses that he does not have this gift should team up with a person or a group who does.

No attempt has been made to champion autocratic or democratic leadership. Frankly, autocratic *vs.* democratic is not the issue here. The issue is helping persons move through change with the least amount of frustration. This can be accomplished by either style of leader if he is people-centered, confident, enthusiastic, and knowledgeable.

The Adoption Process

Persons move through stages of change as they accept a new idea. Joe M. Bohlen and George M. Beal of the Department of Economics and Sociology at Iowa State College discovered in a study of how farm people accept new ideas that they move through five stages of adaptation: (1) awareness, (2) interest, (3) evaluation, (4) trial, and (5) adoption.[24] Experience has taught that these stages are valid whether persons are deciding on a new hybrid corn or a new method of teaching. This outline will be used to discuss the process of accepting a new idea.

Awareness

When a person becomes aware of a new idea but does not know the details, he is in the awareness stage. A person gets this type of information from calendars, news releases, posters, announcements, bulletin boards, newsletters, articles, and many other sources.

The lead time for awareness information depends on the nature of the event. A month lead time may be plenty for a class social, but a year may be needed for a training event at a conference center. The pace at which persons move through this stage of adoption is dependent on the relation of the event to their felt needs.

Interest

The second stage is interest. At this stage a person wants to know the facts about the new idea. He wants to know who, where, what, and how.

The needed information can be carried in flyers, magazine articles, lectures, letters, and news stories. Opportunity for dialogue is good at this stage. Again, lead time depends on the person and the nature of the event.

Evaluation

The evaluation stage occurs when a person assimilates the facts and asks: "What's in it for me? Can I do it? What are the benefits?" A person may continue to rely on printed media, but he also likes to hear testimonies, see demonstrations, and look at samples.

Trial

Now a person is saying: "I want to do it if I can. I'm sold on the benefits." A person must deal with the negative forces that cause him to have difficulty in putting the new idea into practice. Can I do it? Do I have enough time to plan? Will I make a fool of myself?

Obviously, provision of adequate resources, personal encouragement, and an "I'll help you" attitude are important leadership actions here.

Adoption

Adoption completes the process. A person makes it through the trial and adopts the idea as a part of his pattern of actions. He may not use the idea forever, but for now he feels comfortable with it.

Persons move through the process at different rates according to their personalities and the complexity of the situation. Bohlen and Beal say that the simplest category is change in equipment and materials. The second level of complexity is improved practice. Innovation (one change in materials but several changes in practice) is the third level of complexity. Change in the enterprise is the fourth level.

Building a Climate of Stability

Change always involves people. It can be planned or spontaneous. Since change is inevitable and necessary for the renewal of the enterprise, a leader should handle it as wisely as possible. These practical suggestions are given to stimulate thought.

Investigate

Before making plans for change, a leader should thoroughly investigate the need for change, how it will affect persons, and how they feel about it. Only when a leader has armed himself with all the facts of the situation should he plan a new program. Some excellent ideas have been killed because a leader did not do his homework.

The matter of the need for change is the first consideration. Change for the sake of change should be avoided as a general rule. Count the cost of the change. Will the results gained outweigh the potentially disruptive effects? Unfortunately, many programs are launched because of a leader's ego needs rather than the benefit to the mission of the enterprise.

The effect of change on persons is the second consideration. Will the change exceed their capacity for change during a given time period? Realize that as a leader you have a greater desire for and capacity for change. This is especially true if the idea is yours. When change occurs, it affects people. A wise leader not only investigates the need for new programs but also seeks to accurately evaluate the effect of the change on persons.

The ability to listen and understand what is being said is the most important skill of investigation. Factual data and feelings can be gathered. Someone has rightly said, "A person's feelings are real whether they make sense or not." Take some time to listen before developing the plan. The difficulty of communicating the projected change will be cut in half if a leader has sensitively listened to those affected by the change.

Plan

A plan is intended to anticipate and solve problems before they occur. As has already been discussed, persons will resist change more vigorously if the familiar patterns are disrupted and the power structure is disturbed. Almost all change will do this. The best plan is the one that is least disruptive and disturbing. The time to make this judgment is before the change is introduced.

When you hear a person say, "We tried that here and it didn't work," you know that you are dealing with a situation where change was not properly planned and implemented. This is an indication of the "coiled spring" effect. Figure 4 presents this idea graphically. When positive pressure is increased by stressing the "oughts" and neglecting the "can'ts," a negative pressure develops like a coiled spring. As soon as the positive pressure subsides, the spring pushes persons beyond where they were in the beginning. Thus the statement "We tried that and it didn't work." With adequate planning this attitude might not have developed.

Involve persons affected by the change in the development of the plans. The greater the involvement of persons, the greater the ownership. Maximum ownership creates minimum resistance.

Another idea is to keep some of the old to make the new more acceptable. For example, if you are creating new Sunday School departments and adding new classes, leave as many of the existing classes intact as you can. The familiar will offset some of the unfamiliar.

Also, realize that the postchange environment is extremely important to the final outcome of the proposed change. Gellerman believes "the planning of the postchange job environment is actually a more potent de-

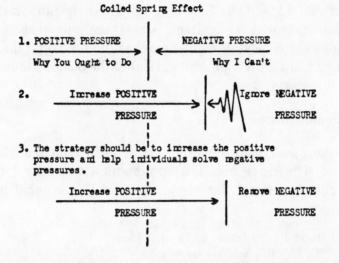

vice for dissolving resistance than group discussion or any other method for the engineering consent." [25]

Timing is important, too. Some men rush in where angels fear to tread. On some occasions leaders are so concerned about getting a new idea across that the capacity of the organization for change becomes saturated. An explosion occurs from doing the right thing at the wrong time.

John was the new pastor of the Green Grass Church. He was committed and excited about the future of the church. In his zeal he introduced a new deacon organization, began a visitation program, added age-division directors in the Sunday School, reorganized the youth program, and started a day-care ministry. He was very disappointed when the church voted down the proposal to revamp the Wednesday schedule. The church had reached the saturation point. A wise leader sets priorities and introduces new ideas as he senses a readiness for the idea. Lyle Schaller, an interdenominational church growth consultant, states that his research shows that most growing churches did not begin their significant growth pattern until after the pastor's fourth anniversary.

Communicate

An apocryphal story is told about a minister who died. His close friend, a sportswriter, was asked to write the epitaph for his tombstone. This is what he wrote:

> Here lie the bones of Brother Jones,
> To him life held no terrors,
> His death was the result of grading adults
> No hits, no runs, just errors.

Helping persons prepare for and implement change can pile up the errors. Communication must be at its best.

First, communicate in advance. Unexpected changes produce fear that control over one's environment is being lost. Fear often produces reaction that is irrational and hostile. Change that works to a person's disadvantage will irritate him. If he is forewarned, at least he does not suffer the fury of helplessness. He also has time to accept the idea psychologically.[26]

As soon as it becomes known that some kind of change is in the works, persons begin to speculate about the effect of the change. At this point a full explanation should be given.

Gellerman speaks the truth when he says, "the longer people speculate in the absence of facts, the more believable their speculations become, until at last the facts may seem like fiction because they are inconsistent with what is already believed." [27]

Legitimize the change with the appropriate persons and groups. A friend of mine has a saying, "There is going to be a grapevine, so put sweet grapes on it." In every situation there are some informal and formal power persons who can communicate good or bad words about the plan. A wise leader knows who these persons are and seeks to keep them in the know.

Allow persons to express their gripes. The capacity to disagree agreeably is desirable for any group. If gripes are not aired, they go underground and become gossip. Gossip usually distorts the truth and makes accurate communication impossible.

Follow Through

Reinforcement of the projected change as it is being implemented is essential. Motivation is usually at its peak as a new program is launched. From that point on, motivation begins to wane. Props are needed to bolster the program as it is implemented. For example, a church visitation plan that started with dozens of persons participating may dwindle to the faithful few in a short time if the idea is not reinforced continually. Visitation honor rolls, announcements of the number who came as a result of visitation, and personal affirmation are examples of the kinds of reinforcement that could be given. Too many leaders feel that their work is done when a program has been launched. Adequate follow-through by action and personal example is absolutely necessary.

7
Key No. 2:
Teamwork

If you need a demonstration of the way a team relationship builds a climate for motivation, make a Friday-night visit to a game at Old City High. Only a few are playing the game, but many others are vitally involved in the experience of the game. The level of motivation ranges from total involvement to passive observation. And some of the most highly motivated persons may be in the grandstands, not on the field. The vicarious involvement of the parents, cheerleaders, student body, and fans may be as highly motivating as playing the game. Also, it is interesting to note the difference in the level of motivation of players and fans when the team is having a winning season.

Achieving a goal generates excitement. The taste of victory builds confidence. Those most highly motivated are those who sense a vital relationship to the mission of the enterprise. The farther removed a person is from the center of the mission, the more difficult it is to build and maintain a high level of motivation. As a rule, the persons who drop out first are those who are on the edge of the action. Team sports are excellent laboratories for a leader to study the motivation of persons.

Key No. 2: Persons are more highly motivated in a climate where they feel themselves to be a vital part of a team with a significant mission.

Teamwork relates primarily to the affiliation need—the need to belong. However, teamwork also interrelates with a person's esteem and achievement needs.

Types of Teams

Teams can be classified as one of two types—ongoing teams with a long-term mission and project teams with short-term missions.

Church committees, Bible study classes, church staff groups, deacon groups, and choirs are just some of the ongoing teams that exist in a typical church.

Temporary committees, task force groups, and study groups are typical types of project teams that churches use.

The concept of creating both ongoing and project teams is certainly not new to church life. In fact, some churches may have created so many teams that some of them do not have a significant mission.

Principles of Good Teamwork

Here are some guidelines for the effective use of teams to build a climate in which persons can be motivated.

Decide on Significant Mission

A few years back the erroneous notion was passed around that a church should have enough committees so that every active church member could serve on a committee. The concept was that putting a person on a committee would ensure a high level of motivation. This is only a half-truth. It is true that persons who are committed to a significant team goal are highly motivated, but many of the expanded committees may not need to meet or they may not have a significant job to do. Thus, the responsibility may be taken lightly and actually become demotivating.

It is definitely not true that placing a person on a team will ensure his or her motivation. If persons are to be motivated by the job, it must be significant. Don't create a team unless there is a significant job to do.

Know Responsibility

Earl Nightingale, a human resources consultant, reports that in one survey nineteen of twenty persons did not know why they went to work each morning. The ratio would probably hold true for persons serving on church teams. Too often those who are enlisting persons for various church responsibilities are so anxious to fill the positions that they consider the job complete when a person says yes. The enlisted person must find out for himself the exact nature of his responsibility.

What a travesty it would be if all of the softball team came to the game expecting to pitch. It can be rather demotivating for team members to be confused about their responsibility. Each team member should know not only his own responsibility but also the work of the other team members. Otherwise, coordination is impossible.

Recognize Importance of Relational Issues

This is particularly true regarding ongoing teams. Time should be spent developing the capacity to work together as a group of diverse individuals. Each person brings his past experiences and his whole personality to the endeavor. In the past, relational issues were often ignored because it was thought to be potentially disruptive to deal with the way persons felt about each other and the task. Today leaders are learning ways to deal with these issues creatively and actually to set ahead the achievement of the assigned task by improving the work environment. Later in the chapter a section is given to team-building techniques.

Leadership Style and Teamwork

The style of a leader can facilitate or hinder a team. For example, a leader who must dominate will usually squelch the creativity of a team. On the other hand, a leader who will not give the team direction will drag the team through the wilderness on the way to the team goal. Figure 5 illustrates three patterns of leadership that a leader may enforce on the group.

Pattern A, The Wheel Model, has a leader who insists that all communication flow through him. This way he can screen and alter the communication. This type of leader is usually very controlling. He tries to keep the lid on conflict. He usually tries to generate most of the ideas and then assign them to various team members for implementation. Team members usually become very dependent on the leader. The style can be very effective if the team leader is extremely creative and has an abundance of energy.

Pattern B, The Four Square Model, is quite different from the Wheel Model. The leader insists that he not be placed in the middle. His major role is to call the team together. The agenda is usually limited to solving coordination problems. His theme is "I'll do my job and you do yours." This is sometimes called the professional model. Each person on the team prides himself on his competence. In fact, the success of this type of team depends upon having highly competent team members. The major problem is that each person on the team operates somewhat independently of the others. Their teamwork is defensive rather than offensive. The style operates best in an organization that is well established and traditional in nature.

Pattern C, the Synergistic Model, is built as an open communication system. The leader accepts the responsibility of giving direction. He insists that the subparts of the organization relate to priorities of the whole. Each member of the team communicates freely with other members. Each team member must wear two hats—one as a member of the team and one as the leader of his organizational subpart. The primary problem of this model is the difficulty of each team member to wear two hats effectively. This requires more meeting time and better group skills. Members must be willing to sacrifice for the good of the whole. The leader must be secure enough to let informal leadership come from any member of the group. It usually takes time for a team to develop this type of work model.

Figure 5

MODELS FOR

TEAM LEADERSHIP

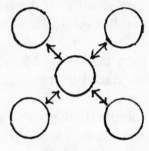

Pattern A
THE WHEEL MODEL

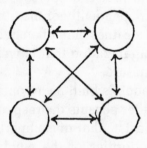

Pattern B
THE FOUR SQUARE MODEL

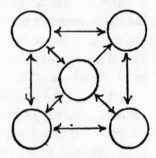

Pattern C
THE SYNERGISTIC MODEL

Setting Priorities

A minister is a part of many teams. In fact, he is a part of so many teams that it becomes very difficult to maintain sufficient relationships to all of the teams. He has a team relationship to the staff, the church council, the deacons, many committees, and the Sunday School council, just to name a few. Almost every hour of the day could be spent meeting with some group.

But how can a minister solve this drain on his time and energy? More effective delegation is part of the solution. However, while serving in an interim capacity several years ago, I discovered a concept that has revolutionized my team relationships.

The concept is that a minister has three levels of team relationships—covenant relationships, equipping relationships, and caring relationships. (See Figure 6.)

Covenant relationships are developed with those five to ten persons with whom a minister is most closely related. For the pastor of a smaller church it could be the heads of the organizations and/or the deacon body. For a pastor of a larger church this may be the church staff. For a church staff member the covenant group would be the close associates that he relates to organizationally. The covenant relationship is a deep one and is purposefully developed. It is built on mutual respect and personal commitment. The relationship begins with a one-to-one commitment. The minister should take the initiative to establish the covenant. Let's suppose he is privately talking with John, the Sunday School director. The conversation may go like this:

"John, if this church achieves all that God needs and wants it to, you and I are going to have to work closely together as a team. I believe we must establish a covenant with each other to be friends, to pray for one another, to support the other in times of crises, and to be open and honest in our dealings. When we don't agree, let's talk it out between ourselves rather than taking our case to other church members. I'll never say anything behind your back. I'll never intentionally do anything to hurt you. I don't expect you to always support my ideas in public or private, but I want the kind of personal relationship to you so that you will not doubt and can support my motives.

I am willing to make this covenant to you. Can you make it to me?''

This excerpt of a hypothetical conversation is not meant to be a script for such a covenant. It is given because it seems to be the easiest way to communicate the idea and the depth of commitment involved.

A covenant relationship requires personal commitment and continuing maintenance. Weekly and sometimes daily contact is needed. Time must be spent dreaming, planning, and celebrating together. It is because of the depth of commitment and the time required to maintain the relationship that a person must limit this level to five to ten persons. Although the commitment must first be made personally, the entire team can also enter into an appropriate covenant.

The equipping level of team relationships involves more persons and is much broader in scope. This level of team relationship involves the elected leaders of the various organizational units. For a pastor or a minister of education, this would include the teachers and officers of the church organization. Although some of these persons may be close personal friends with whom a minister would have a covenant relationship, from an organizational point of view the relationship of level would not involve a one-to-one covenant. The emphasis is on equipping. The minister would seek to provide the training, counseling, and resources needed for the person to be effective and personally fulfilled. There would be many personal relationships, but not on the depth of the covenant group. Small groups would provide the primary setting for this relationship.

The caring level of team relationship involves the entire congregation. This level would major on contact in congregational services, crises ministry, and significant celebration times.

This concept views the church as a network of teams. Ideally, every member of the church should be involved in a covenant team. A covenant relationship offers the greatest satisfaction for a person's affiliation needs. For some, a Bible study class should offer a covenant relationship. For others the relationship to the fellow teachers and officers in a department would provide the setting. Fortunately, many church groups are discovering the joy of a covenant relationship.

Also, the concept does not seek to place quality limitations on each encounter that a minister has with persons to whom he relates. A minister will give his best, whether relating to the Sunday School director or a marriage counselor. The concept relates to the amount of time, type of mutual support, and limit of intention for various organizational relationships. It acknowledges the fact that a minister cannot be all things to all persons to whom he relates.

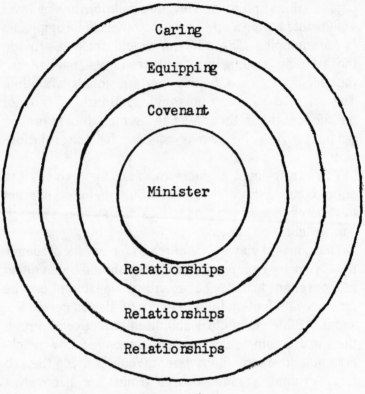

Figure 6

PRIORITIES IN GROUP RELATIONSHIPS

Building a Climate of Teamwork

A team relationship seldom just happens. An effective team is put together by deliberate effort. Maintenance is required, too. The following actions are needed to build and maintain an effective team.

Contract

Accepting an organizational position may formally make a person a team member, but it certainly does not create a team relationship with other team members. If the team is to be effective, some form of contracting among members is needed. The contract need not be written, but it should be as specific as possible. The contract should include both task and personal data.

It is at this point that persons spell out their expectations. The verbal contract becomes a foundation for the life and work of the group. Someone has wisely said, "Where there is no understanding, there is misunderstanding." Unfortunately, too many groups ignore this action.

Contracting is also very important regarding a person's affiliation needs. A sense of belonging is heightened through a process of contracting. The action should be done when the group forms and when each new member is inducted. The presentation of a list of duties may serve as a task contract. The conversation regarding the establishing of a personal covenant presented earlier in this chapter is an example of a personal contract. This could be adapted for group use.

Share

The sharing of personal history is the second action in team building. Until group members get to know one another, they cannot develop mutual respect and appreciation. Sharing of personal histories may be done informally as a group forms. As a new member joins, this can be repeated. The Quaker dialogue has been used by many groups. The dialogue is a series of four questions:

1. Where did you live between the ages of nine and twelve?

2. What was the center of physical warmth during this period?

3. What was the center of human warmth?

4. When did God become more than a word to you?

Sharing will continue as a team builds a spirit of togetherness. The depth of sharing will increase as trust builds among team members. Intercessory prayer will become a vital part of the group relationships.

Affirm

As the team members become better acquainted, affirmation should become a vital part of their experience. Affirming and supporting the other team members is a particularly excellent source of satisfying belonging needs. The essence of belonging occurs when other group members appreciate the personal qualities and skills of a team member.

Someone has said that every Christian should be a minister of affirmation. He should affirm God's handiwork in other persons he meets. After all, God often uses other persons to reveal himself to us.

One minister says he tries to affirm some work of God in another person each day. He reports that the

Holy Spirit has often led him to a person who desperately needed affirmation on a particular day.

Interact

As a team develops trust and acceptance, responsible two-way communication will increase. This can only happen when the team members feel a level of personal acceptance that will enable them to speak honestly without fear of destroying the relationship. The word *responsible* is important. Interaction that is responsible builds respect. Tactless confrontation can destroy team spirit. The use of effective group dynamics skills by the team leader can greatly facilitate healthy interaction.

The willingness of a team to mold together their best thinking indicates a good level of maturity. Each member must give and take in order to find the best solution. Challenges are not considered a personal affront. Responsible interaction creates a keen sense of belonging. It says: "My opinions are important. I'm needed."

Celebrate

A team should take time to celebrate together. Too often team members become so task-oriented that they forget to take time to savor the good things that God is doing among them. The psalmist said, "Sing praises to the Lord, which dwelleth in Zion: declare among the people his doings" (Ps. 9:11). To celebrate means more than just affirming another person's good work. Celebration is rejoicing together in the Lord. Some church staff teams, for example, get together at the pastor's home at regular intervals to celebrate the good things that are happening and to praise God for his goodness.

A team that practices these actions will be highly motivated. Each member will own his stake in the organization and its mission. Team members will feel a sense of belonging to a group who care about one another and are committed to achieving its mission.

8
Key No. 3: Affirmation

The adage says that an ounce of prevention is worth a pound of cure. In human dimension this truism could be changed to: An ounce of affirmation is worth a pound of criticism or ten pounds of indifference.

The issue is self-esteem—how does a person feel about himself or herself? A person's self-image is a controlling factor in a person's life. Persons tend to act out the way they feel about themselves.

Although self-esteem is defined as how a person feels about his own worth, a person usually builds these feelings from the signals received from other persons.

What a terrible sin it is to put another person down. What a joy it is to affirm another person. This is the essence of Christian leadership—helping persons discover and channel the gifts that are within them. Every

Christian leader needs to see himself or herself as a minister of affirmation.

Key No. 3: Persons are more highly motivated in a climate where their sense of self-worth is affirmed and enhanced.

A Leader's Self-Esteem

The leader's own self-esteem is the key to his ability to help others improve their sense of security. A leader with a high degree of self-esteem exhibits confidence. He can think about the needs of others because he does not have to compete with them to meet his own needs.

What a leader believes about himself influences his ability to trust his followers. Persons with high self-esteem tend to have a high expectation of persons who report to them. They are usually willing to trust their workers to do their job.

Building a Climate of Affirmation

Affirmation is at the heart of the Christian ministry. To be effective in this arena of leadership requires more than a few handy-dandy motivational gimmicks. To be an effective affirmer requires a leader to put his own needs aside and be very sensitive to the needs of others. Effective affirmation is as much a style of life as it is a method of leadership. Unfortunately, many manipulative gimmicks parade under the banner of giving recognition and affirmation.

Effective, genuine affirmation reqiures an interlinking of four leader actions: acceptance, trust, reward, and support.

Acceptance

John had grown up in the church. He was a happy-go-lucky kid who created havoc in almost every Sunday School class he attended. No one really took John seriously when he began in his early twenties to ask each year to be given some responsibility in Sunday School. When his name was mentioned in the nominating committee, persons would say, "Not John, he couldn't control the class." But one man didn't feel that way. Fred, a department director, asked that he be allowed to contact John about a position. He saw in John a quality of leadership that was needed in his department. John is now a deacon and a Sunday School department director. He delights in taking young men whom others do not want to accept and guiding them in Christian growth.

The ability to see the potential in another person and to respect him as a person of worth is the first step toward affirmation. Respect means to have a "we" attitude. We are in this together. Each of us has something to contribute to the relationship and the work. Respect means genuine appreciation of another person. Although respect is often communicated verbally, it is also easily communicated nonverbally. In fact, some leaders destroy their credibility by verbally praising someone while nonverbally putting him down.

Personal attention also shows acceptance. Allotting time to a person shows that you consider him and his work important. If you cannot find time to give personal attention to a worker, he may decide that you do not consider his work important. He may begin to lose interest.

A pastor of a small, beginning church shared how he had rejoiced when a well-educated, experienced worker had joined his church. But much to his displeasure, the worker had not gotten into the mainstream of church life. After analyzing the situation in a motivation conference, the pastor decided to give the man his personal attention. Several months later the pastor reported that the person had caught fire and was now the Sunday School director.

Personal attention says, "You are important."

Different persons need differing amounts of personal attention, too. For some persons a monthly coffee break is sufficient. Other persons require weekly meetings. A leader must be sensitive to the needs of his associates and try to relate to them accordingly. Obviously, good principles of time management must also be a concern.

Involvement of another person in decision making is the height of acceptance. By involvement a leader is not only saying *I respect you as a person,* but also *I appreciate your ideas.* In other words, *I need you.*

By involving other persons in problem analysis and decision making, better information will likely be generated. Persons will feel greater ownership of the decision and will likely be more committed to its implementation.

It was Jack's usual practice to plan the agenda for the annual church leader retreat. Frankly, because he had run out of ideas, he decided to involve the workers in a brainstorming session about the retreat agenda.

He could not believe the ideas that came forth when he felt his barrel was dry. He was even more pleased with the pride of ownership that developed.

Involvement is time consuming. Obviously, a leader cannot make all decisions by group involvement. He must pick those that are most appropriate.

Trust

The second dimension of creating a climate of affirmation is trust. Trust is a common, simple word but a powerful word. Trust means giving responsibility. For many persons responsibility is the most motivating condition in their life. They thrive on the challenge of being in charge of some operation.

Numerous research projects have demonstrated that a person's progress and growth in a job depends largely on his leader's expectation.

Mrs. Cotton was the director of a Children's department. While the church as a whole was generally looking for workers to staff the Sunday School, Mrs. Cotton had a waiting list of persons to work in her department. Her department was the only one in the Sunday School that had an effective weekly planning meeting. Mrs. Cotton made it clear that workers were expected to attend the planning meetings, visit their assigned group, and be present every Sunday. Her expectations were high, but her workers responded.

Unfortunately, leaders often are more effective in communicating low expectations than high. What leaders say matters less than what they do. Expectations are communicated more frequently by nonverbal signals. The example a leader creates by his actions often becomes the norm. High, realistic expectations demonstrate trust and affirmation.

Closely linked to expectations is delegation. Delegation means to trust a person enough to put him on his own. Until a leader is willing to let a person make and learn from his mistakes, he is not ready to delegate.

It is not easy for a leader to let go. He may have a special attachment to a particular type of work and find it most difficult to let another person have the reins.

Jim was the only pastor the Holly Springs Church had had in its twelve-year history. The church had grown—especially the youth program. Jim had given much attention to this area. Now the church had called Joan to be the church's youth director. Unfortunately, Jim did not realize his problems in delegating until Joan had resigned. A pastor-friend helped him see his difficulty and correct it.

Trusting a person enough to delegate a task or an area of work is a significant affirmation.

Paul was the Church Training director. The annual workers' banquet was coming up, and the pastor asked him to handle the arrangements. However, the pastor told Paul when, where, and how to have the dinner. In fact, the pastor even suggested the menu. The pastor obviously thought he was being helpful. The pastor was surprised when he learned that Paul had come by the office and dumped the whole affair on the church secretary. He said something like this to the secretary: "I don't know why he asked me to do this."

A person's feeling of affirmation is greatly heightened

by the freedom to make his own decisions. This is particularly true when delegating to a person who is a decision maker in other areas of his life. The limits of freedom need to be tailored to the person involved.

Delegation without accountability says that the job is not important. If the outcome of a job is not important enough to a leader to check on the results, there is a good chance it is busywork. Accountability gives a type of status. Give the persons who did the job an opportunity to report on it.

Church committee work is a good example. At the beginning of the church year the election of committee members and the handing out of duties is a big thing. But the committees are never asked to report unless a crisis occurs. It is no wonder that few committees function properly. Look at the committees and other groups such as deacons that are highly motivated. These will be the groups that make regular reports to the congregation. They feel accountable. Accountability increases the amount of affirmation that a person receives from a job.

Reward

Everyone needs to know that his work is appreciated. The larger the organization, the more blurred a person's contribution becomes. The loss of personal identity is discouraging. It is very important to see that persons are rewarded for work well done. There are several ways to reward persons: praise, status, and freedom for more independent action.

Praise from a leader is especially important because

it represents a pat on the back from someone in authority. Some leaders cheapen their use of recognition by overusing it and by giving it when it is not really merited. This becomes embarrassing and demotivating.

Private praise is often more affirming than public praise. A person knows that the leader is not giving the recognition to receive praise himself. Leaders need to be cautious that public and private recognition is not used to manipulate persons.

This has been called a generation of status seekers. While status can be taken to an extreme, it remains a primary way to reward a person. Titles, ranks, and awards are formal ways that a leader can bestow status. However, the sharing of visibility is an often overlooked way that can be very motivating. In essence, sharing visibility such as platform leadership is sharing a part of a leader's status. The leader must obviously be secure enough in his own self-esteem to share his status. However, it is also true that by sharing status a leader often gains prestige in the eyes of his congregation. People appreciate a person who is willing to share power.

The specific ways to provide status are numerous. Here are a few:

1. Provide badges for ushers.

2. Designate a deacon of the week in the church newsletter.

3. Ask different persons to participate in the leadership of the worship service.

4. Designate a person (or persons) to officially represent you at a function you cannot attend.

5. List in the newsletter the names of persons who are leaders of various organizations.

6. Let persons make announcements regarding their organization rather than doing it yourself.

7. Design a distinctive logo and slogan for the church that can be used on buses, newsletters, T-shirts, and so on.

8. Provide uniforms for the church custodians (unless you're the custodian).

9. Send workers to training events.

10. Formally elect substitute teachers and officers.

Support

Acceptance, trust, and reward are not complete without support.

Tim was elected director of a Youth department. He was a very gifted person. He had served in several positions and had completed numerous training courses. He began the new year with great enthusiasm. His department had weekly planning meetings. He worked hard to make sure everything was just right for Sunday morning. But after about three months his enthusiasm began to wane. Planning meetings stopped. Within six months he was missing about one Sunday per month because of family activities. His teachers were complaining about his lack of preparation. One teacher had resigned and Tim had combined two classes.

Does this sound familiar? Tim's motivation dropped below zero. Why? One very important reason is that he did not receive supervision and support from the

Sunday School director and the staff. Tim is one of those persons who can't operate without support. Three ways to provide support are: coaching, constructive feedback, and backup.

A football coach would not think of placing a player in a position, giving him a manual about his position, and turning him loose to play the game. This is exactly what many church leaders do. Coaching means guiding. It means observing a person's performance and providing the proper training to sharpen his skills. Coaching is counseling. A worker should feel free to ask advice of his coach.

Coaching is a skill that many leaders need to learn. A good coach does not solve the problem for the person. He helps the person solve his problem by asking questions, providing data, and analyzing facts. It is surprising how much a person will grow in his work with effective coaching.

It is also important for a coach to not insist that his players be a mirror of him. Each person is an individual with his own strengths and gifts. An effective coach will try to help a person develop his own individuality.

Coaching involves goal setting. Charles had taken the time at the beginning of the year to work with each department director to set goals for his department. After six months, one of the directors began to get slack in his work. The worker quickly corrected his own behavior when Charles asked how his department was coming on the goals and whether they would be on target by the end of the year.

Constructive feedback is another way to provide support. Persons want to know where they stand. They deserve honest feedback from the leader. Leaders sometimes avoid criticism because they fear the person will be hurt. Usually the hurt is worse if the person hears the leader's evaluation from someone else.

The most difficult situation a leader faces is discussing a performance problem with the worker. The discussions have a way of getting personal and painful. Such confrontations are sometimes necessary and must be handled delicately. A good rule to remember is to confront the problem, not the person. Have a "we" attitude. If an Adult department director has not followed through with visitation as was agreed, approach the director by saying, "What can I do to help you get the visitation plan rolling?" Don't say, "Jim, why have you folks not followed through on the visitation plan?"

Handle problems promptly. Some leaders seem to follow a strategy of ignoring a problem and hoping it will go away. Sometimes it may go away, but more often it continues to fester and grow. Many serious problems could have been solved easily if they had been handled promptly.

Nothing is more devastating to the morale of a worker than to be left out on a limb by his staff leader. Someone has said, "Stand by your workers, and they will stand by you." This does not mean that you should endorse the mistakes of a worker. But you should refrain from engaging in criticism of him. When someone brings a criticism to you, try to help him understand the strengths of the person he is criticizing. By all means, don't make an agreement with a worker and then fail to stand by it when someone from the power structure seeks to be critical of him.

Jesus has set the example by showing great affirmation toward his disciples. To a person they each had their faults, but Jesus affirmed their great value to him and to God. In Jesus' prayer in John 17, he prayed, "Holy Father! Keep them safe by the power of your name . . . so that they may be one as you and I are one" (v. 11). "I do not ask you to take them out of the world, but I asked you to keep them safe from the Evil One" (v. 15). In another passage he promised that he would never forsake them and that no man could take them from him. When Peter proclaimed that Jesus was the Messiah, Jesus said, "Good for you, Simon, son of John" (Matt. 16:17, TEV).

I believe Jesus also says, "Good for you," when we affirm in his children the gifts that he has placed within them. Good for you, pastor! Good for you, church staff member! Good for you, Sunday School leader! An ounce of affirmation is worth a pound of criticism and ten pounds of indifference.

9
Key No. 4:
Challenge

The principal character of the cartoon is a roach. The script begins as a moth stops to ask the roach if he knows where he can find a fire. The roach replies, "Why are you looking for a fire?" The moth answers, "I must find a fire I can burn up in." "Well, if you must find a fire, there is one just down the street," says the roach. So the moth flies down the street into the fire and burns up. As the roach watches in disbelief, his first response is, "What a waste." But his second response is prophetic. He says, "Oh, that I was committed enough to something that I would be willing to burn up in it."

Being motivated enough to some ideal or objective to be willing to "burn up in it" is the highest level of motivation. As noted previously, Abraham Maslow calls this self-actualization. Maslow, unlike many other psychologists, built his work around research with emotionally normal persons. Through his investigations he discovered that within each person there is a need to grow, achieve, and be committed to a significant cause.[28]

The apostle Paul is an excellent example of a self-actualized person who was totally committed to his calling. In Philippians 3:13-14 he vigorously declared his commitment to his mission: "Of course, brethren, I really do not think that I have already reached it; the one thing I do, however, is to forget what is behind me and do my best to reach what is ahead. So I run straight toward the goal in order to win the prize, which is God's call through Christ Jesus to the life above" (TEV).

Maslow defines a self-actualized person as "an exceptional person who is primarily motivated by the need to develop and actualize his fullest potentialities and capacities." [29]

Key No. 4: Persons are more highly motivated in a climate where they are challenged to develop their full potential and to commit their energies to meaningful ideals and objectives.

Few persons are able to expend a significant amount of their energies in pursuit of growth needs. Tragically, many persons are so preoccupied with lower needs that they never experience the joy of self-actualization.

Persons who are motivated significantly by their growth needs march to the beat of a different drummer. Their physical, security, affiliative, and esteem needs are being relatively well met. External stimuli are seldom needed for them to be highly motivated. They have an inner compulsion to grow and achieve.

To build an environment of challenge that will call forth the self-actualization in persons is a leader's highest calling.

The Profile of a Self-Actualizer

Before moving to a discussion of building a climate of challenge, a profile of a self-actualizing person is needed to clarify the concept more fully.

Committed to a Specific, Meaningful Mission

Without exception self-actualizing persons are dedicated to some work, duty, or vocation which they consider important. The work toward these ends is both exciting and pleasurable. Commitment is unyielding. The self-actualizer strives to do his work well and is willing to work very hard to achieve the goal.[30]

Concentrates on Concerns Outside of Self

Self-actualized persons are not self-centered persons. They concentrate on problems external to themselves. They are persons with a world view.[31]

Paul illustrated this attitude very well when he said, "So I become all things to all men, that I may save some of them by any means possible" (1 Cor. 9:22, TEV).

Capable of Meaningful Relationships

Self-actualizers, says Maslow, are capable of more love and deeper relationships than most people.[32] Their healthy self-esteem is obviously an undergirding strength at this point. They have confidence in themselves and are not easily threatened by other persons.

Self-actualizers usually do not have a large number of close personal friends because they are more concerned about the mission than about socialization. At times they may even appear aloof. But the friendships they have are usually deep and meaningful.

Perceives Issues Clearly

Self-actualizers see issues clearly. They have a clearer notion of right and wrong than the average person. They are far above average in their ability to judge other persons. With their superior perception they can see concealed and confused realities quickly and accurately. Again the ability rests firmly on their healthy sense of security and self-esteem. They do not waste energy with the reactions of others to their action. This ability allows a self-actualizer to solve problems quickly and efficiently.

Spontaneous and Direct

A spontaneous, natural style is another personal trait of a self-actualizer. His open, uninhibited, expressive manner makes him come across as very real and authentic. He is not artificial.[33] He has no need to put on airs. On some occasions a self-actualizer may even appear abrupt because of his directness. He is a readable person because his positions on issues are usually well known. Spontaneity and directness give him credibility.

Courageous in the Face of Opposition

The superior sense of self-worth that a self-actualizer has also allows him to take risks an average person would not take. He is willing to stand for his beliefs against opposition. His values are usually based on his own perceptions rather than on what others tell him. Maslow states that all of the great creators he studied "testified to the element of courage needed in the lonely moment of creation, affirming something new (contradictory to the old)." [34] Self-actualizers are open to new ideas and are willing to risk opposition if the idea is of value to them.

Confident in Self

Strength is a visible characteristic of a self-actualized person. He has a minimum of self-conflict. His confidence is based on the knowledge that he is a competent, adequate person. This enables him to give more energy to being a productive person. He does not need to spend time protecting himself from himself. His superior self-confidence enables him to resist outside pressures and to maintain a certain inner detachment. [35]

Positive Attitude Toward Life

Self-actualizers do not dwell on the negative. Although they are not immune to fears and anxieties, they refuse to be pessimistic. [36] This attribute enables a self-actualizer to enjoy life and to give positive reinforcement to others. Other persons are attracted by his optimistic spirit.

Capable of Deep Spiritual Experience

Although Maslow was not studying the religious practices or capacities of self-actualizers, he discovered that a great number of them had peak experiences, mystical experiences, oceanic feelings, and feelings of limitless horizons opening up before them.[37] They believed in a meaningful universe and a life which could be called spiritual.

Building a Climate of Challenge

If self-actualization is such a worthy goal, how does a leader help persons to discover and enjoy this level of motivation? The strategy must be twofold. First, a leader should seek to help persons satisfy their safety, social, and esteem needs. Unless these needs are relatively well met, a person cannot meaningfully pursue his growth needs. Second, a climate of challenge is needed to activate the growth aspirations of persons.

Since the three previous chapters dealt with helping persons meet safety, social, and esteem needs, the remaining part of this chapter will discuss the matter of challenge. Five approaches provide the climate of challenge: (1) project a challenging vision, (2) be an example of faith, (3) help persons set specific goals, (4) call forth gifts of persons, and (5) direct the endeavor courageously.

Project a Challenging Vision

"Where there is no vision the people perish" (Prov. 29:18). Visionary leadership is absolutely necessary for helping persons reach their highest motivational potential. Effective leaders have always been persons who could dream dreams. Edward Lindaman, a Christian futurist, says that "if you can imagine it, it can come true."

The attitude of a leader about future possibilities can ignite the enterprise to achieve greatness. The story of the two shoe salesmen who visited Africa illustrates the importance of a leader's being optimistic about future possibilities. One of the salesmen sent a telegram to his company: "Cancel my order for shoes; nobody over here wears shoes." The other salesman saw a completely different picture. He wired his company: "Double my order; everyone over here needs shoes."

I recently spoke with a pastor who has been very effective in leading the churches he has pastored to accomplish great goals and asked him to tell me the secret to his effective leadership. His reply was, "I try to dream big dreams and believe they can be achieved."

Just to be able to dream great dreams himself, however, is not sufficient. A leader must be able to help others become visionary. He must be able to communicate the joy of dreaming dreams and seeing visions. The ability to verbalize his own dreams and to help others get their dreams in concrete form is an essential part of the climate of challenge.

Be an Example of Faith

John Bisagno, pastor of the First Baptist Church, Houston, Texas, says the Lord has given him the gift of faith. With his leadership this great church is achieving many worthy goals. He means by this statement that with God's help anything is possible. An attitude of faith in God's power is a second element that is needed before one can become a self-actualizer.

James Evans, pastor of the First Baptist Church, Santa Fe, New Mexico, says: "A vision without a task is only a dream; a task without a vision is boredom; but a task with a vision is the hope of the world."

Paul said, "I can do all things through Christ which strengtheneth me." An atmosphere of faith and confidence in the power of God awakens in persons the gift of faith that is within them. The ability of a leader to project this type of confidence depends upon his own relationship of faith. A strong personal devotional life provides the foundation.

Help Persons Set Specific Goals

A climate of challenge is dependent upon persons' understanding where they are going and how they intend to get there. An effective leader must help persons set and accept specific goals that will lead toward the achievement of the dream.

Goals are essential to good planning. They offer the following helps for planners:

- Provide a specific challenge toward which the church can concentrate its attention and resources.
- Help persons to visualize in specific terms what the church intends to accomplish for Christ in a given period of time.
- Affect the number and type of activities a church

can plan to accomplish. A goal to reach five men for Christ requires much less planning and work than a goal to reach five hundred men.

- Affect the way the church uses its time, personnel, finances, and facilities. Reaching five men with the gospel is not nearly as costly as reaching one thousand men.

Goals should be sound and challenging. They should be based on factual evidence. They should be attainable. Goals should include the following:

A statement of desired results.—What does the church really want to accomplish? Means and methods should be reflected later in action plans. Goals should only reflect intended results.

A statement of quality or quantity.—Goals should be measurable objectively or subjectively. Goals are intended to provide a means of evaluating the effectiveness of the church's work. Therefore, they should contain a measurable quantity or quality.

A statement of time.—Goals should have a completion date. Because dates act as milestones for a working church, they should be reflected in goals.

Grant Teaff, Baylor University's head football coach, is a great believer in helping persons to set growth goals. Each coach and player puts his goals on index cards and files them with the coach. They are reviewed twice a year by the person and Teaff. An example of the motivating power of personal goals is vividly portrayed in the story that Coach Teaff relates about Aubrey Schulz.

Early in 1974 Aubrey Schulz handed me his goal card. He was a reserve lineman who weighed only 210 pounds and didn't play enough to letter as a junior in '73 when we were 2-9. I looked at his card and said, "Aubrey, you have a high goal here." He said, "Yes, sir, I sure do." "I see where you want to be all-Southwest Conference center next season." "Yes, sir, I sure do." "That's strange since you play guard." "Yes, sir, I know, but I want to play center and I thought if I put it among my goals that you would . . . ah . . . would . . . ah . . . change me." I said, "Okay. We'll think about it."

I looked again and saw another goal. It was, of all things, to be all-American center! Then I looked and saw a third goal: To help lead Baylor to a conference championship!

We hadn't been conference champions in fifty years and didn't win a conference game in 1973, and he's going to lead us to a championship! Well, I'm as positive as anybody but I thought that was a little unrealistic. But I didn't say so. I started talking to him about how he was going to attain these goals.

First of all, I told him he must gain a lot of weight. "If you're playing center when we open at Oklahoma next September you'll have to block a nose guard who weighs 250 pounds. Everyone else through the schedule will be as big or bigger, going up to 290, Louie Kelcher at SMU."

He said, "Coach, I want to play. I want to win. I'll do whatever it takes." Well, we put him on a training program and I've never seen a guy work harder. In spring practice he became our starting center but he still weighed only 218 pounds. He kept working on the program though and I told him to call me in the middle of the summer and tell me how he was doing. He had a job in a pizza restaurant

and he tried to eat all the pizza there. He did every-
thing to gain weight. He called me and said, "Coach
Teaff, you won't believe it but I weigh 221!" I said,
"Three pounds. That's great! That's advancement!
Come on it bigger." "Yes, sir," he said.

When we started 2-a-day workouts in the fall he
weighed 223. He was fantastic. I've never seen anybody work any harder, develop techniques any better. We opened with Oklahoma and after the game
their starting nose guard was benched. Next week
at Missouri we lost again in the fourth quarter but
he played great. Then we came home to play Oklahoma State, eighth-ranked in the nation and with
a 280-pound nose guard. Aubrey now weighed 229
pounds and he whipped him all over the field. We
won by 17 points.

The rest of the season we lost one game. We won
the Southwest Conference championship and Aubrey Schulz, who was considered the eighth best
center in an eight-team league in September, was
the unanimous choice for all-Southwest Conference.
And when the Football Writers of America named
their all-America squad, Aubrey Schulz was first
team. Even more fantastic, after we ended the regular season November 30 by beating Rice to clinch
the championship, I put him on the scales. He
weighed 245 pounds.

I'll never see a better example of a guy bringing
his goals alive. Aubrey Schulz decided where he
wanted to go and he was able to put wheels to
those goals.[38]

Call Forth Gifts of Persons

God has not given a mission that he has not made
available the resources to achieve. Within each church
God has placed the gifts needed to get the job done.

A major role of a leader is to help persons discover their gifts and commit them to service. Unfortunately, many persons are dormant. Too many persons are sitting on the sidelines. Some are there because they are apathetic. Others need help to discover and channel their unique gifts. In Ephesians 4 Paul described the church as the body of Christ. Each part of the body has one or more functions to perform. Each part is needed to make the body complete.

Effective leaders help persons discover who they are as persons in Christ, recognize their God-given abilities, and celebrate these gifts in his service.

A leader nurtures a person until he has the skill and confidence to apply the potential God has placed in him. Someone has said, "A person must crawl before he can walk, and walk before he can run." A climate where total stewardship of life is taught and total mobilization of personal gifts is expected will lead to greater involvement in achieving the dreams and goals.

Direct the Endeavor Courageously

The final action of challenge is courageous leadership. Every army needs a field general. His responsibility is to direct the troops to effectively carry out their strategy. He may be out front urging the troops to follow him into battle, or he may be behind the lines laying out tactics for the next day's encounter.

Contrary to popular opinion, a leader does not have to be an autocrat. An autocratic leader seeks to get persons to accept and follow his ideas without question. Anyone who questions the leader is brought into submission or purged. A developmental leader can be just as effective. He involves persons in decision making. He has ideas, but he is willing to change or to adapt when a better way is found. He is sensitive to the needs of persons. The leader personifies the mission. He becomes the visible symbol of the conquest. Without courageous leadership the vision is only a dream.

Conclusion

While building a climate for motivation is the key to helping persons become motivated, the four keys don't tell the whole story. There is a fifth key—prayer. Prayer is a mystical ingredient of motivation that cannot be explained by visible cause and effect. Jesus said, "Ask, and it shall be given to you; seek, and you shall find; knock, and it shall be opened to you" (Matt. 7:7, NASB).

Prayer does change things. Prayer is not just an action to take when all else fails. Prayer should permeate all that is done to provide a climate of stability, teamwork, affirmation, and challenge.

The power of prayer is awesome. The Spirit of God intercedes in ways not describable in words. Romans 8:26 says, "And in the same way the Spirit also helps our weakness; for we do not know how to pray as we should, but the Spirit Himself intercedes for us with groanings too deep for words" (NASB).

While prayer should not be a last resort, a Christian can know that when persons do not respond to the best efforts to help them become motivated, God has promised to hear and answer prayer. "Therefore I say to you, all things for which you pray and ask, believe that you have received them, and they shall be granted you" (Mark 11:24, NASB). Fervent, intercessory prayer is the fifth key to effective motivation. And while God expects a Christian leader to vigorously put feet to his prayers, the task cannot be done in his own strength. We are "God's fellow workers" (1 Cor. 3:9, NASB). What a promise! "If God be for us, who can be against us?" (Rom. 8:31).

Notes

1. From the *New American Standard Bible.* Copyright ©
The Lockman Foundation, 1960, 1962, 1963, 1971, 1972, 1973,
1975. Used by permission. Subsequent quotations are marked
NASB.

2. Martin Luther King, Jr., *The Measure of a Man* (Philadelphia: Pilgrim Press, 1968), p. 26.

3. From *The Bible in Today's English Version.* Old Testament: Copyright © American Bible Society 1976. New Testament: Copyright © American Bible Society 1966, 1971, 1976.
Used by permission. Subsequent quotations are marked
(TEV).

4. E. Y. Mullins, *The Christian Religion in Its Doctrinal
Expressions* (Philadelphia: Judson Press, 1917), p. 255.

5. William L. Hendricks, *The Doctrine of Man* (Nashville:
Convention Press, 1977), pp. 47-48.

6. Ibid., p. 48.

7. Mullins, *The Christian Religion,* p. 258.

8. Hendricks, *The Doctrine of Man,* p. 28.

9. Abraham Maslow, *Motivation and Personality* (New
York: Harper & Row, Inc., 1970), p. 39.

10. Saul Gellerman, *Motivation and Productivity* (New York:
American Management Association, 1963), p. 155.

11. Maslow, *Motivation and Personality,* p. 41.

12. Ibid., p. 43.   13. Ibid., p. 45.

14. Frank G. Gable, *The Third Force* (New York: Pocket
Books, 1971), p. 42.

15. Paul Hersey and Kenneth H. Blanchard, *Management*

of Organizational Behavior: Utilizing Human Resources (Englewood Cliffs: Prentice-Hall, Inc., 1977), p. 32.

16. Gable, *The Third Force,* p. 42.

17. Maslow, *Motivation and Personality,* p. 47.

18. Ibid.

19. Gable, *The Third Force,* p. 48.

20. Hersey and Blanchard, *Organizational Behavior,* p. 43.

21. Everett L. Shostrom, *Man, the Manipulator* (New York: Bantam Books, 1968), pp. 3-4.

22. Ibid., p. xii.

23. Maslow, *Motivation and Personality,* pp. 35-57.

24. Joe M. Bohlen and George M. Beal, "The Diffusion Process, Agriculture Extension Service Special Report No. 18" (Ames: Iowa State University, 1957), p. 2.

25. Gellerman, *Motivation and Productivity,* p. 265.

26. S. E. Stevens, *Overcoming Resistance to Change* (Chicago: Dartnell Corporation, 1965), p. 10.

27. Gellerman, *Motivation and Productivity,* p. 264.

28. Gable, *The Third Force,* pp. 23-36.

29. Ibid., p. 24.   30. Ibid., p. 27.

31. Colin Wilson, *New Pathways in Psychology* (New York: Mentor Books, 1974), p. 155.

32. Ibid., p. 156.

33. Gable, *The Third Force,* p. 28.

34. Abraham Maslow, "The Need to Know and the Fear of Knowing," *The Journal of General Psychology,* 1965, p. 68.

35. Wilson, *New Pathways,* p. 155.

36. Ibid., p. 157.   37. Ibid.

38. Grant Teaff, *I Believe* (Waco: Word Books, 1976), pp. 33-35.